Index to

Montgomery County, Tennessee,

Wills and Administrations

1795 to 1861

Byron and Barbara Sistler

JANAWAY PUBLISHING, INC.
2013

Index to
Montgomery County, Tennessee,
Wills and Administrations, 1795 to 1861

Originally published, Nashville, 1986

Reprinted for
Byron Sistler and Associates, Inc.

by

Janaway Publishing, Inc.
2412 Nicklaus Dr.
Santa Maria, California 93455
(805) 925-1038
www.JanawayGenealogy.com

2007

ISBN: 978-1-59641-135-7

Made in the United States of America

INDEX TO
MONTGOMERY COUNTY, TENNESSEE
WILLS & ADMINISTRATIONS 1795 TO 1861

The index covers all will books and record books from 1795 through 1861. The entries were taken directly from microfilm of the original books. They are relatively self-explanatory, but a few observations are in order:

The year shown is, where possible, year of the probate. Otherwise year of the will, or first year mention is found of the estate.

At the end of each entry is identification where the instrument can be found--wb (will book) or rb (record book) followed by book # and page number. For example, rb-g-445 means Record Book G page 445.

In general we attempted to insert notation regarding an estate only once, when it first appeared in the records. Exceptions were (1) if there was an actual will, the page number was shown even if there was a previous entry for that estate; (2) if a later insertion had been found with a more complete name--name instead of initials, etc.--or a substantially different spelling of what seemed to be the same name; (3) if ten years or more had passed since last entry for that name.

Guardian proceedings and settlements are to be found sprinkled throughout the books. While these contain much data of genealogical value, we omitted these references as not within the scope of this particular work.

Where a book had two series of pagination--starting over with page 1 somewhere in the middle, for example--we have marked the second set of page numbers with an asterisk.

Byron Sistler
Barbara Sistler

August 1990

Achey, D. 1855 rb-o-2
Achey, Jacob 1836 rb-g-445
Adam, Robert 1819 rb-c-184
Adams, Caroline 1840 rb-i-5
Adams, Catharine 1842 rb-i-392
Adams, Eleanor (Mrs) 1858 rb-o-585
Adams, Elener 1856 rb-o-20
Adams, James 1819 rb-c-73
Adams, John 1821 rb-c-455
Adams, R. H. 1832 rb-f-447
Adams, Richard 1827 rb-e-177
Adams, Richard H. 1837 rb-g-497
Adams, William C. 1854 wb-n-219
Adams, Benjamin 1817 rb-b-404
Adams, David 1831 rb-f-304
Adams, Edwin H. 1829 rb-e-510
Adams, James 1839 rb-h-216
Adams, Thomas 1829 rb-e-484
Albright, John 1827 rb-e-133
Alcock, Jane 1820 rb-c-389
Allen, A. W. 1858 rb-o-567
Allen, John 1828 rb-e-300
Allen, John J. 1827 rb-e-57
Allen, Richard 1845 rb-j-378
Allen, A. W. (Mrs.) 1858 rb-o-541
Allen, Alexander M. 1837 rb-g-620
Allen, Drury 1850 rb-l-630
Allen, George 1847 rb-k-486
Allen, James 1845 rb-j-456
Allen, Valentine 1840 rb-i-2
Allen, Valentine 1857 rb-o-509
Allensworth, Priscilla E. 1861 rb-p-612
Alley, Miles 1818 rb-c-83
Alley, Samuel 1836 rb-g-480
Alley, Samuel sr. 1838 rb-h-41
Allison, James 1841 rb-i-212
Allman, James 1858 rb-o-659
Ally, James 1818 rb-c-39
Alsup, Martha 1857 rb-o-429
Alwell, Thomas 1856 rb-o-224
Anderson (B), Garland 1850 rb-l-615
Anderson, Daniel 1819 rb-c-74
Anderson, Elijah 1816 rb-b-323
Anderson, Garland 1850 wb-m-20
Anderson, James 1853 wb-n-68
Anderson, John C. 1850 wb-m-78

Anderson, Thornberry 1824 rb-d-369
Anderson, Timothy 1817 rb-b-398
Anderson, Samuel W. 1845 rb-k-26
Anderson, Thornsbury 1824 rb-d-375
Andrews, Baker 1836 rb-g-416
Andrews, Benjamin 1847 rb-k-481
Anglin, Caleb 1856 rb-o-257
Anthony, William B. 1827 rb-e-251
Apperson, Albert 1838 rb-h-173
Apperson, Albert A. 1838 rb-h-151
Apperson, Jacob 1822 rb-d-23
Apperson, Jacob 1831 rb-f-177
Apperson, Jacob 1832 rb-f-328
Apperson, William R. 1842 rb-i-429
Applewhite, Rebeccah 1835 rb-g-181
Archey, D. A. 1856 rb-o-33
Armfield, Jacob 1815 rb-b-280
Armstead, Martin 1859 rb-p-182
Armstead, Robert 1853 wb-n-164
Armstead, Robert sr. 1859 rb-p-112
Armstead, Robert 1853 wb-n-170
Atchey, D. A. 1855 wb-n-607
Atkins, Margaret 1860 rb-p-427
Atkinson, Joshua 1846 rb-k-229
Atwell, Thomas 1857 rb-o-440
Averett, Henry W. 1857 rb-o-492
Averett, Nancy 1836 rb-g-331
Averitt, Washington 1853 wb-n-143
Baggatt, John 1857 rb-o-354
Baggett, Henry 1815 rb-b-283
Baggett, John 1815 rb-b-281
Bagwell, G. P. 1847 rb-k-545
Bagwell, John W. 1846 rb-k-302
Bagwell, Nicholas E. 1835 rb-g-184
Bagwell, Pleasant 1846 rb-k-332
Bagwell, Drury 1841 rb-i-202
Bagwell, Julia 1843 rb-j-39
Bagwell, Samuel 1825 rb-d-428
Bailey, Gala 1846 rb-k-215
Bailey, Henry 1816 rb-b-309
Bailey, Henry L. 1848 rb-l-1
Bailey, Hiram 1850 wb-m-125
Bailey, Jacob 1844 rb-j-83
Bailey, Jesse 1857 rb-o-287
Bailey, Lucinda 1851 wb-m-386
Bailey, William S. 1828 rb-e-252

Bailey, Wm. 1855 wb-n-522

Bailey, Benjamin 1785 rb-c-357

Bailey, Jessee 1857 rb-o-290

Baily, Pollie 1858 rb-o-702

Baily, Zachariah 1844 rb-j-214

Baine, Daniel 1820 rb-c-354

Baker, John E. 1845 rb-j-356

Baker, Nancy (Mrs.) 1833 rb-f-477

Baker, Nancy 1831 rb-f-257

Baker, John 1830 rb-f-38

Baker, John sr. 1827 rb-e-140

Baker, Nancy 1831 rb-f-303

Baker, William 1815 rb-b-258

Ballard, John 1861 rb-p-554

Ballentine, David 1850 rb-l-548

Barbee, Augustus 1846 rb-k-306

Barbee, John 1856 rb-o-176

Barbee, A. C. 1854 wb-n-492

Barber, John 1855 wb-n-641

Barker, Alexander M. 1830 rb-f-21

Barker, Edward S. 1840 rb-i-31

Barkesdale, Thomas W. 1857 rb-o-487

Barnes, Mary 1844 rb-j-124

Barnes, Mathew 1811 rb-a-497

Barnes, Thomas H. 1840 rb-h-406

Barnes, Joseph 1839 rb-h-291

Barnes, Reps 1821 rb-c-463

Barns, Repp 1827 rb-e-79

Barret, Elizabeth 1847 rb-k-613

Barret, Sampson 1845 rb-j-449

Bartin, Bradly 1856 rb-o-168

Barton, William 1820 rb-c-364

Barton, William jr. 1818 rb-b-512

Barton, John 1855 wb-n-583

Barton, William 1825 rb-d-465

Basford, James 1826 rb-d-522

Batson, Alexander 1857 rb-o-368

Batson, Elizabeth 1859 rb-p-152

Batson, Francis 1831 rb-f-153

Batson, Thomas 1831 rb-f-201

Batson, Thos. H. 1861 rb-p-650

Baxter, Robert 1850 rb-l-635

Baxter, Robert sr. 1850 wb-m-34

Baxter, Theodore 1861 rb-p-646

Baxter, Robert 1851 wb-m-403

Bayless, Burrell 1827 rb-e-174

Bayless, John 1836 rb-g-416

Bayless, Joseph P. 1840 rb-h-390

Bayless, Robert 1840 rb-h-389

Bayless, Burrell 1828 rb-e-201

Bayless, John 1810 rb-a-381

Bayliss, Patience 1859 rb-p-183

Beasley, James 1843 rb-i-506

Beaumont, F. S. 1861 rb-p-646

Beaven, E. L. 1852 wb-m-501

Beck, Edward 1850 wb-m-16

Beck, Patsy 1835 rb-g-99

Bell, Bayard T. 1835 rb-g-231

Bell, David 1805 rb-a-258

Bell, Regard? T. 1855 wb-n-574

Bell, Bayard T. 1840 rb-h-441

Bellamy, John 1860 rb-p-493

Bennett, Mason 1816 rb-b-330

Berry, Edwin 1828 rb-e-272

Bevil, Allan 1834 rb-f-571

Bevil, Mann? 1832 rb-f-395

Bevil, Mary 1834 rb-f-571

Bevils, Robert 1815 rb-b-76

Bigger, Robert 1837 rb-g-633

Bird, Genny 1847 rb-k-460

Bird, Jerry 1846 rb-k-231

Bird, John 1825 rb-d-522

Black, Peter 1856 rb-o-22

Black, Robert 1841 rb-i-148

Black, Saml. 1835 rb-g-214

Blair, John H. 1850 wb-m-99

Blair, John M. 1848 rb-l-137

Blair, Susan (Mrs) 1848 rb-l-166

Blair, Thomas B. 1848 rb-l-130

Blair, James H. 1860 rb-p-406

Blair, John 1828 rb-e-370

Blair, Susan 1848 rb-l-129

Blair, Thomas B. 1836 rb-g-441

Blakemore, George M. 1847 rb-k-418

Blakemore, George N. 1848 rb-l-109

Blakeney, Harriet 1823 rb-d-183

Blakeney, James 1823 rb-d-155

Blakeney, Thomas 1841 rb-i-88

Blakeney, Thomas 1822 rb-d-38

Blakeny (B), Harriet 1823 rb-d-89

Blakney, Thomas 1840 rb-h-455

Blanks, William 1806 rb-a-372

Blanton, Richard 1803 rb-a-156

Blount, Willie 1836 rb-g-264

Boardman, Margaret M. 1860 rb-p-314

Bobo, Hiram 1830 rb-f-114

Bobo, Love C. 1842 rb-i-225

Bobo, Hiram 1831 rb-f-186

Boon, John 1834 rb-g-63

Booth, Mark 1858 rb-o-713

Boothe, Pleasant 1856 rb-o-128

Borlieu, Nathan 1846 rb-k-258

Bostelle, John 1823 rb-d-238

Bournes, Benjamin F. 1857 rb-o-373

Boutell, John 1824 rb-d-309

Boutelle, John jr. 1828 rb-e-278

Bowers, Andrew 1861 rb-p-580

Bowers, James 1860 rb-p-513

Bowers, W. 1847 rb-k-678

Bowers, Wm. 1847 rb-k-482

Bowles, Rewben 1844 rb-j-264

Bowles, Thomas E. 1841 rb-i-193

Bowles, Thomas E. 1845 rb-j-393

Bowling, Gabriella C. 1853 wb-n-199

Bowling, W. W. 1851 wb-m-332

Bowling, J. P. 1859 rb-p-225

Bowling, W. W. 1851 wb-m-378

Bowling, Wm. 1851 wb-m-319

Boyd, George 1835 rb-g-98

Boyd, George C. 1847 rb-k-561

Bradberry, Ann E. 1845 rb-j-321

Braime, James 1847 rb-k-643

Brantley, Eliza J. 1858 rb-o-672

Brantley, James 1810 rb-a-344

Brantley, James 1845 rb-j-344

Brantley, Lewis 1856 rb-o-68

Brantley, Lucy 1850 wb-m-151

Brantley, Naomi 1854 wb-n-372

Brantley, Thomas 1814 rb-b-177

Brantley, William 1841 rb-i-104

Brantley, Charles 1803 rb-a-180

Brantley, Hugh 1856 rb-o-62

Brantley, Thomas 1814 rb-b-180

Brantly, Neander 1854 wb-n-341

Brantly, Neona 1856 rb-o-186

Brantly, Abraham 1850 wb-m-106

Breeden, John 1854 wb-n-228

Brenin, William 1836 rb-g-274

Brickle, Jeremiah 1837 rb-g-513

Brien, William 1835 rb-g-211

Briggs, Elizabeth M. 1849 rb-l-333

Brigham, James 1815 rb-b-77

Bristow, John 1848 rb-k-801

Bristow, John 1848 rb-l-15

Britt, Zedakiah 1856 rb-o-216

Britt, Zedekiah 1859 rb-p-264

Britton, William T. 1852 wb-m-460

Brodie, John 1830 rb-f-140

Broom, Brittain 1815 rb-b-278

Brown, Alexander 1814 rb-b-193

Brown, Andrew 1861 rb-p-528

Brown, J. W. 1847 rb-k-521

Brown, James 1834 rb-f-541

Brown, Jeremiah 1838 rb-h-170

Brown, Joel M. 1849 rb-l-474

Brown, John 1838 rb-h-77

Brown, John W. 1837 rb-h-21

Brown, Mary 1848 rb-k-702

Brown, Polly 1848 rb-k-734

Brown, Wm. M. 1855 wb-n-688

Brown, James 1848 rb-l-96

Brown, Lockey 1825 rb-d-479

Brown, Silviah 1834 rb-g-159

Brown, Silvy 1852 wb-m-538

Bruce, W. K. 1861 rb-p-597

Bruce, Wm. H. 1861 rb-p-637

Brumfield, Nancy 1828 rb-e-379

Brumfield, Obediah 1825 rb-d-499

Brumfield, Obediah 1829 rb-e-431

Brunson, Asahel 1815 rb-b-277

Brunson, Asahel 1828 rb-e-205

Brunson, Penelope 1832 rb-f-337

Brunson, Asahel 1828 rb-e-358

Bryan, Asa 1839 rb-h-248

Bryan, Asa M. 1847 rb-k-513

Bryan, Asa N. 1836 rb-g-334

Bryan, Dennis 1837 rb-h-20

Bryan, R. H. 1858 rb-o-703

Bryan, Hardy 1825 rb-d-427

Bryan, Henry H. 1835 rb-g-222

Bryan, William 1831 rb-g-290

Bryant, Asa N. 1846 rb-k-266

Bryant, Hardy 1825 rb-d-418

Bryarly, Tate 1852 wb-m-618

Buck, John L. 1850 rb-l-585

Buck, John L. 1840 rb-i-1

Buck, Peter C. 1861 rb-p-624

Buckley, Thomas M. 1848 rb-k-703

Bull, Balaam 1839 rb-h-335

Bull, Jeremiah 1815 rb-b-210

Bull, John 1856 rb-o-221

Bull, Randal 1818 rb-a-469

Bullard, R. N. 1835 rb-g-285

Bullard, Reben N. 1836 rb-g-271

Bullard, Rueben 1835 rb-g-212

Bullard, Reuben N. 1838 rb-h-152

Bumpass, Elizabeth 1846 rb-k-144

Bumpass, Gemima 1851 wb-m-76

Bumpass, John 1835 rb-g-251

Bumpass, John 1850 rb-l-590

Bumpass, Lucy Ann 1842 rb-i-323

Bumpass, Nancy 1837 rb-h-12

Bumpass, Nancy 1858 rb-o-723

Bumpass, Samuel 1831 rb-f-255

Bumpass, Samuel 1850 wb-m-4

Bumpass, Samuel T. 1832 rb-f-314

Bumpass, Samuel 1831 rb-f-299

Bumpass, Samuel 1836 rb-g-465

Bunnell, James C. 1853 wb-n-88

Bunting, David 1846 rb-k-303

Bunting, David 1858 rb-o-549

Bunting, James A. 1811 rb-b-3

Burgain, John 1806 rb-a-89

Burney, W. L. 1858 rb-o-745

Burney, David 1852 wb-m-429

Burney, Dicie 1858 rb-o-717

Burress, David 1805 rb-a-273

Burress, George H. 1829 rb-e-493

Burress, George H. 1829 rb-e-511

Bush, Zenas 1829 rb-f-64

Byrd, John 1815 rb-b-304

Byrd, John 1828 rb-e-255

Cage, Alfred 1850 rb-l-623

Cage, Edward 1859 rb-p-143

Cahorn, William 1834 rb-f-557

Cain, E. G. 1841 rb-i-125

Cain, Elisha G. 1843 rb-i-487

Caldwell, David 1835 rb-g-256

Caldwell, John 1836 rb-g-337

Caldwell, John Jr. 1843 rb-i-549

Caldwell, John sr. 1825 rb-d-487

Caldwell, Robert 1825 rb-d-414

Caldwell, Samuel sr. 1841 rb-i-136

Calhoon, William 1835 rb-g-286

Calhoon, William 1838 rb-h-65

Call, H. A. 1852 wb-m-553

Campbell, Elizabeth 1826 rb-e-3

Campbell, John 1813 rb-b-99

Caraway, Thomas 1835 rb-g-107

Carlyle, Sarah 1854 wb-n-343

Carnes, John 1812 rb-b-119

Carney, James 1839 rb-h-208

Carney, James M. 1834 rb-g-70

Carney, James W. 1835 rb-g-160

Carney, Richard (Genl.) 1832 rb-f-416

Carney, Richard 1831 rb-f-219

Carney, Sally W. 1842 rb-i-228

Carney, Stephen W. jr. 1860 rb-p-478

Carney, Thomas L. 1831 rb-f-220

Carney, Thomas L. 1849 rb-l-476

Carney, James W. 1837 rb-g-602

Carney, James Wright 1825 rb-d-466

Carney, Richard 1834 rb-g-41

Carney, Sally 1819 rb-c-210

Carney, Thomas 1849 rb-l-331

Carns, John 1824 rb-d-374

Carny, William 1856 rb-o-211

Carr, James 1837 rb-g-491

Carr, James 1839 rb-h-247

Carroll, John 1852 wb-m-610

Carroll, William 1846 rb-k-105

Carter, John 1842 rb-i-373

Carter, Robert 1848 rb-l-145

Castelbury, Paul 1815 rb-b-265

Castleberry, Sampson 1836 rb-g-388

Castlebury, Paul 1815 rb-b-281

Chambless, Mark 1841 rb-i-103

Chambless, Mark 1841 rb-i-105

Chamell, Thomas F. 1854 wb-n-457

Channel, Elisha J. 1855 wb-n-680

Channell, Elisha 1806 rb-a-302

Channell, Elisha 1853 wb-m-646

Channell, Henry S. 1852 wb-m-464

Chapman, Benjamin 1832 rb-g-68

Charnell, Henry S. 1838 rb-h-87

Cherry, S. M. 1855 wb-n-689

Cherry, Charles 1819 rb-c-82

Cherry, Charles 1822 rb-d-74

Chessenhall, Meredith 1857 rb-o-514

Chester, Minerva 1859 rb-p-54

Chiles, Hendy Ann 1855 wb-n-712

Chiles, Henry 1836 rb-g-503

Chiles, Henry T. 1836 rb-g-476

Chiles, Joseph 1860 rb-p-311

Chisenhall, Virlen 1855 wb-n-599

Chisenhall, Reuben 1829 rb-e-509

Clardy, James 1841 rb-k-300

Clark, Isaac 1859 rb-p-57

Clark, George 1849 rb-l-450

Clark, Mary 1857 rb-o-289

Clarke, Henry 1856 rb-o-210

Clements, Agnes 1820 rb-c-361

Clements, William 1822 rb-d-33

Clifton, Henry E. 1846 rb-k-253

Clifton, Edwin 1826 rb-e-2

Clinton, Elizabeth 1860 rb-p-471

Cobb, Hannah 1828 rb-e-259

Cobb, William 1803 rb-a-168

Cobbs, John H. 1834 rb-g-65

Cochran, Simeon 1851 wb-m-193

Cock, Hartwell B. 1836 rb-g-444

Cock, Henry 1847 rb-k-370

Cock, Nancy 1836 rb-g-344

Cock, Sarah G. 1837 rb-g-619

Cock, Mary 1845 rb-j-300

Cocke, Abraham 1830 rb-f-18

Cocke, Elizabeth B. 1819 rb-c-264

Cocke, Richard 1823 rb-d-155

Cocke, Stephen 1829 rb-f-4

Cocke, Susan 1836 rb-g-443

Cocke, William Batt 1814 rb-b-175

Cocke, Abraham 1815 rb-b-75

Cocke, Abraham 1817 rb-b-456

Cocke, Elizabeth 1817 rb-b-454

Cocke, Nancy 1837 rb-g-512

Cocke, Peter 1803 rb-a-198

Cohoon, William 1832 rb-f-307

Coldwell, John 1823 rb-d-254

Cole, Henry A. 1851 wb-m-275

Cole, Peter H. 1824 rb-d-300

Cole, Peter H. 1836 rb-g-409

Cole, Peter 1823 rb-d-253

Colelough, Grisby 1843 rb-i-451

Coleman, James 1859 rb-p-245

Coleman, Turner 1836 rb-g-390

Coleman, Braxton 1832 rb-f-447

Coleman, Rice 1853 wb-n-140*

Colishaw, John 1859 rb-p-33

Collier, Ardelia 1858 rb-o-604

Collier, Daniel 1821 rb-c-401

Collier, Thomas 1857 rb-o-495

Collier, Thomas Sr. 1859 rb-p-271

Collier, James M. 1844 rb-j-82

Collins, John R. 1825 rb-d-473

Collins, Maria 1834 rb-g-25

Collins, Mary 1859 rb-p-279

Collins, Nathan 1838 rb-h-124

Collins, John R. 1825 rb-d-477

Collins, Robert 1857 rb-o-380

Collins, William 1838 rb-h-112

Colman, James 1850 wb-m-62

Conner, Samuel F. 1831 rb-f-238

Conner, Samuel T. 1832 rb-f-382

Connery, Samuel T. 1831 rb-f-211

Conrad, W. W. 1854 wb-n-218

Conrad, Joseph 1795 rb-a-2

Cook, William 1858 rb-o-766

Coon, James 1836 rb-g-470

Coon, James 1850 wb-m-129

Coon, James W. 1853 wb-n-59

Coon, James sr. 1848 wb-m-63

Cooper, Alice G. 1858 rb-o-711

Cooper, Howard? 1830 rb-f-36

Cooper, John 1809 rb-a-429

Cooper, Robert 1854 wb-n-433

Cooper, Susan Tennessee 1858 rb-o-775

Cooper, Tennesee 1858 rb-o-715

Cooper, Vincent 1845 rb-j-392

Cooper, Esther 1820 rb-c-315

Cooper, Hiram 1829 rb-e-485

Cooper, Richard 1857 rb-o-315

Corban, William 1827 rb-e-199

Corbin, Charnall 1823 rb-d-124

Corbin, Joseph 1825 rb-d-448

Corbin, William jr. 1807 rb-a-458

Corby, Timothy 1860 rb-p-354

Cording, Jacob 1843 rb-j-17

Corely, Jucy? Jane 1855 wb-n-639

Corlew, William sr. 1841 rb-i-171

Cossett, Lucinda 1848 rb-l-158

Councel, David 1823 rb-d-213

Council, Dudley 1848 rb-l-115

Council, Morris 1856 rb-o-250

Council, Willis 1848 rb-l-127

Council, Elizabeth 1852 wb-m-578

Cowhard, Jno. W. 1847 rb-k-745

Cowherd, R. C. 1850 wb-m-60

Cox, Andrew 1805 rb-a-252

Cox, H. 1849 rb-l-465

Coyle, Francis 1850 rb-l-540

Creath, Mary 1823 rb-d-208

Creath, Samuel 1823 rb-d-239

Creath, Samuel 1823 rb-d-251

Creswell, James 1815 rb-b-244

Creswell, Samuel 1812 rb-b-30

Crockett, James 1847 rb-k-437

Crockett, Judge W. 1852 wb-m-432

Cromwell, Catharine L. 1846 rb-k-299

Crotzer, Jacob 1844 rb-j-103

Crouch, Harden 1846 rb-k-113

Crow, Polly 1802 rb-a-158

Crowder, Miles 1837 rb-h-11

Crowder, John H. 1857 rb-o-336

Cruse, Robert H. 1853 wb-n-107

Cummings, Aaron 1861 rb-p-556

Cummings, James 1861 rb-p-556

Cummins, David H. 1834 rb-f-544

Cummins, Jacob B. 1848 rb-l-180

Cummins, Sally 1833 rb-f-426

Cupboy, Timoty 1860 rb-p-385

Curl, Wilson 1803 rb-a-167

Cuthbertson, Jessee 1854 wb-n-558

Cuthbertson, John 1811 rb-b-8

Cuthbertson, Jessee 1855 wb-n-569

Dabney, E. J. (Mrs.) 1856 rb-o-56

Dabney, E. J. 1855 wb-n-498

Dabney, Frances 1846 rb-k-326

Dabney, J. T. 1847 rb-k-578

Dabney, John T. 1833 rb-f-520

Dabney, Mildred 1846 rb-k-269

Dabney, Samuel (Dr.) 1835 rb-g-101

Dabney, William H. 1836 rb-g-389

Dabney, Elizabeth 1852 wb-n-512

Dabney, Samuel 1829 rb-e-402

Dade, Lucien 1855 wb-n-593

Dailey, Richard 1832 rb-f-336

Dailey, Richard 1848 rb-l-7

Dailey, Richard E. 1846 rb-k-118

Daley, William 1858 rb-o-542

Dance, John 1829 rb-f-14

Daniel, R. H. C. 1858 rb-o-631

Daniels, William 1857 rb-o-441

Daniels, William 1857 rb-o-442

Darden, Patience 1829 rb-e-404

Darnell, Benjamin 1815 rb-b-249

Darr, Daniel 1831 rb-f-235

Daughton, M. M. 1849 rb-l-505

Daughton, Molder M. 1850 rb-l-547

Davidson, Absolom 1856 rb-o-60

Davidson, John 1802 rb-a-151

Davie, James 1847 rb-k-651

Davie, James 1858 rb-o-572

Davie, Jones 1860 rb-p-337

Davie, Kendal 1834 rb-g-28

Davie, John 1830 rb-f-21

Davie, Jones 1847 rb-k-431

Davie, Kendal 1834 rb-g-61

Davis, Absalom 1854 wb-n-484

Davis, David 1838 rb-h-150

Davis, David 1861 rb-p-619

Davis?, John 1830 rb-f-84

Davis, Absalom 1835 rb-g-108

Davis, Charles 1850 rb-l-594

Davis, Isaac 1839 rb-h-349

Davis, James 1847 rb-l-134

Davis, James 1857 rb-o-290

Davis, Robert 1859 rb-p-135

Davis, Samuel 1826 rb-e-32

Dawson, Absolum 1854 wb-n-430

Dawson, L. 1832 rb-f-331

Dawson, Willis L. 1828 rb-e-329

Dawson, Stephen N. 1856 rb-o-33

Dear, John 1799 rb-a-43

Deavenport, Rebecca 1846 rb-k-44

Denning, N. A. 1860 rb-p-441

Dennis, Marmaduke D. O. 1854 wb-n-378

Dennis, Zebedee 1839 rb-h-347

Dennison, Ellen Mary 1845 rb-j-429

Dennisson, Isaac 1841 rb-i-168

Dick, William 1851 wb-m-388

Dickson, F. H. 1848 rb-k-794

Dickson, Hugh 1839 rb-h-195

Dickson, Hugh 1841 rb-i-92

Dickson, Joseph 1839 rb-h-349

Dickson, William 1847 rb-k-661

Dikes, John 1813 rb-b-112

Dikus, John 1812 rb-a-73

Dillard, James 1835 rb-h-435

Dilliard, Luke 1817 rb-b-418

Dilliard, Luke 1828 rb-e-305

Dilliard, Ally 1833 rb-f-464

Dinwiddie, Robert C. 1851 wb-m-391

Dodd, Thomas sr. 1850 wb-m-87

Dodd, Thomas 1850 wb-m-30

Dolun, Elizabeth 1859 rb-p-208

Dortch, Isaac 1828 rb-e-271

Dortch, J. B. 1847 rb-k-680

Dortch, James M. 1846 rb-k-207

Dortch, James N. 1846 rb-k-274

Dortch, James jr. 1848 rb-l-104

Dortch, John B. 1833 rb-f-485

Dortch, Norflett 1854 wb-n-431

Dortch, John B. 1834 rb-g-72

Dortch, Martha 1855 wb-n-637

Dotson, John 1843 rb-i-508

Doughton, Charles 1832 rb-f-370

Douglass, Robert 1860 rb-p-406

Dudley, J. B. 1860 rb-p-514

Dudley, John B. 1861 rb-p-548

Dudley, R. B. 1860 rb-p-428

Dudley, Benjamin Howard 1833 rb-f-503

Duff, Barny 1819 rb-c-77

Duff, Mary 1834 rb-g-21

Duke, A. H. 1837 rb-h-17

Duke, Amos H.? 1832 rb-f-367

Duke, E. L. 1856 rb-o-188

Duke, Elias G. 1835 rb-g-186

Duke, Elizabeth S. 1853 wb-n-98

Duke, John 1819 rb-c-215

Duke, Louisa S. 1860 rb-p-334

Duke, Philip 1835 rb-g-234

Duke, Prudence P. 1851 wb-m-217

Duke, Rebecca 1815 rb-b-298

Duke, Sarah 1859 rb-p-34

Duke, Phillip 1837 rb-g-581

Duke, Prudence P. 1838 rb-h-120

Duke, Robert 1845 rb-j-406

Dukes, John 1803 rb-a-178

Dunbar, Ann 1824 rb-d-296

Dunbar, Thomas 1824 rb-d-396

Dunbar, Thomas 1810 rb-a-491

Dunlavy, Sallie 1858 rb-o-538

Dunning, N. A. 1860 rb-p-348

Durr, Daniel 1831 rb-f-155

Durrett, J. W. 1858 rb-o-633

Durrett, James W. 1858 rb-o-686

Durrett, W. H. 1858 rb-o-663

Dycus, John 1830 rb-f-140

Dycus, Edward 1858 rb-o-676

Dye, B. R. 1861 rb-p-629

Dye, Benson W. 1859 rb-p-152

Dye, George W. 1850 wb-m-121

Edes, Jessee 1844 rb-j-65

Edmonds, Benjamin 1854 wb-n-434

Edmondson, Benjamin 1855 wb-n-525

Edmonston, Ardas? 1830 rb-f-17

Edmonston, Robert 1799 rb-a-31

Elder, James 1826 rb-e-82

Eldridge, Edwin H. 1858 rb-o-603

Eleazer, John 1819 rb-c-78

Eleazer, George 1815 rb-b-273

Eleazor, Catharine 1843 rb-i-551

Elliot, William 1836 rb-g-320

Elliott, Margarett 1837 rb-g-498

Elliott, William 1822 rb-d-16

Elliott, William 1855 wb-n-694

Elliott, Wm. J. 1846 rb-k-81

Elliott, Elizabeth 1854 wb-n-554

Elliott, James 1816 rb-b-267

Elliott, Lewis 1810 rb-a-435

Elliott, Nancy 1811 rb-b-36

Elliott, William 1832 rb-f-333

Ellison, James 1853 wb-m-645

Ely, Jessee 1847 rb-k-390

Epps, Daniel 1813 rb-b-106

Evans, Isaac H. 1859 rb-p-200

Everett, John D. 1848 rb-k-757

Everit, John 1821 rb-c-430

Ewing, H. L? 1858 rb-o-637

Ewing, H. Q? 1859 rb-p-258

Ezell, Henry 1859 rb-p-279

Fairmon, John 1810 rb-a-350

Falkner, John 1820 rb-c-336

Farear, William 1810 rb-a-364

Farley, William 1841 rb-i-74

Farley, William M. 1839 rb-h-195

Farrier, Mary 1813 rb-b-340

Farrier, Mary 1824 rb-d-391

Faulk, Alford 1836 rb-g-403

Faulk, William 1830 rb-f-142

Faulkner, John (Capt) 1818 rb-c-11

Faulkner, John sr. 1818 rb-b-511

Faulkner, William 1822 rb-d-47

Faulkner, William 1827 rb-e-254

Faulkner, William 1832 rb-f-355

Fawley, Elizabeth 1831 rb-f-206

Fawley, William 1828 rb-e-368

Feas, Charles 1798 rb-a-26

Feasly, Lucy 1848 rb-l-86

Fentress, James 1843 rb-i-550

Ferguson, Elizabeth 1856 rb-o-244

Ferman, John 1809 rb-a-470

Flemming, Joseph B. 1824 rb-d-294

Fletcher, Abram 1855 wb-n-672

Fletcher, Catharine 1858 rb-o-744

Fletcher, Henry 1859 rb-p-296

Fletcher, M. V. (Mrs.) 1859 rb-p-40

Fletcher, Mary V. 1859 rb-p-16

Fletcher, Thomas 1835 rb-g-67

Fletcher, William 1845 rb-j-404

Fletcher, William T. 1845 rb-j-353

Fletcher, Abram 1855 wb-n-679

Fletcher, Henrietta 1846 rb-j-469

Fletcher, John 1814 rb-b-219

Fletcher, Lydia M. V. 1861 rb-p-614

Fletcher, Thomas 1835 rb-g-71

Fletcher, Winnie 1859 rb-p-282

Flimmon, Joseph B. 1826 rb-d-532

Flowers, Alexander 1847 rb-k-412

Flowers, Orlando 1845 rb-j-324

Flowers, C. 1853 wb-n-3

Foalk, William 1830 rb-f-108

Folks, Martha 1827 rb-e-68

Ford, James 1808 rb-a-102

Ford, Judith 1812 rb-b-118

Ford, John P. 1812 rb-b-52

Ford, Judah 1812 rb-b-83

Forkner, John 1814 rb-b-174

Forsythe, John 1843 rb-i-516

Fort, Jacob H. 1845 rb-j-322

Fort, James 1819 rb-c-182

Fort, James 1845 rb-j-322

Fort, John 1836 rb-g-428

Fort, John D. 1830 rb-f-19

Fort, Charles 1845 rb-k-27

Fort, William A. 1817 rb-b-386

Fort, William A. 1844 rb-j-442

Fortson, Catharine 1857 rb-o-353

Fortson, Marshall 1824 rb-d-397

Fortson, John 1832 rb-f-386

Fortson, Mildred 1822 rb-d-93

Fortson, Richard 1832 rb-f-400

Fortson, William 1843 rb-i-547

Fortune, A. R. 1842 rb-i-303

Foster, Anthony C. 1816 rb-b-333

Foster, H. B. 1854 wb-n-225

Foster, Hiram 1857 rb-o-467

Fowkes, John 1823 rb-d-153

Fowler, Nancy 1809 rb-a-470

Fowler, William 1815 rb-b-296

Fowler, James 1856 rb-o-39

Frazier, Thomas W. 1847 rb-k-503

French, John 1796 rb-a-4

French, John B. 1833 rb-f-471

French, John sr. 1807 rb-a-449

French, Samuel S. 1816 rb-b-358

French, Thomas J. 1841 rb-i-147

French, J. B. 1833 rb-f-465

French, John 1829 rb-e-482

Frost, Ebenezer 1825 rb-d-469

Funk, Henry 1839 rb-h-266

Gabbe, James 1857 rb-o-503

Gable, Jacob 1850 wb-m-105

Gaby, William 1848 rb-k-711

Gage, John 1837 rb-h-13

Gainer, John 1803 rb-a-182

Gainer, Sally 1819 rb-c-181

Gaines, John 1803 rb-a-198

Gains, Abraham C. 1857 rb-o-366

Galbraith, John 1845 rb-j-462

Ganter, John 1851 wb-m-390

Gardner, Mary L. 1850 rb-l-628

Gardner, Warren 1839 rb-h-336

Gardner, Mary L. 1850 rb-l-629

Garland, H. S. 1845 rb-j-414

Garret, Isaac 1825 rb-d-428

Garrett, Martin 1818 rb-b-509

Garrot, Jacob 1826 rb-e-49

Garth, W. A. 1844 rb-j-144

Gee, Joseph 1823 rb-d-244

Gelligher, John 1827 rb-e-225

Gibbert, William 1837 rb-g-618

Gibson, Alexander 1835 rb-g-223

Gibson, Edwin 1829 rb-f-2

Gibson, Edwin 1845 rb-j-298

Gibson, Mary 1832 rb-f-327

Gibson, Philander 1841 rb-i-187

Gibson, Susan 1828 rb-e-378

Gibson, William R. 1828 rb-e-328

Gibson, Wilson 1829 rb-f-2

Gibson, Edwin 1830 rb-f-53

Gibson, John 1828 rb-e-369

Gilbert, William 1837 rb-g-567

Gilbert, Mary 1847 rb-k-389

Gillespie, James 1817 rb-b-458

Givens, Hannah 1853 wb-n-163

Givins, Hannah 1853 wb-n-161

Gleaves, Michael 1811 rb-a-514

Glenn, William 1841 rb-i-154

Glenn, Nathan 1839 rb-h-323

Golliday, Gorge 1817 rb-b-460

Gonsalus, Daniel 1804 rb-a-231

Gordan, Robert B. 1854 wb-n-434

Gorden, Charles H. 1846 rb-k-216

Gordon, William 1814 rb-b-206

Goss, Fredrick 1811 rb-b-4

Goss, Frederick 1822 rb-d-65

Gowans, John 1830 rb-f-93

Goyne, James 1838 rb-h-93

Grace, Soloman sr. 1829 rb-e-403

Grady, Ann (Warfield) 1840 rb-h-472

Grafton, R. L. 1861 rb-p-560

Grant, Charles 1824 rb-d-298

Grant, Charles 1852 wb-m-500

Grant, James 1859 rb-p-123

Grant, Joshua 1849 rb-l-511

Grant, Joshua D. 1850 wb-m-126

Grant, Mary R. 1860 rb-p-329

Grant, Burrel 1824 rb-d-399

Grant, Charles 1824 rb-d-300

Grant, James 1859 rb-p-130

Grant, Mary M. 1853 wb-n-168

Gray, George 1847 rb-k-591

Gray, James 1816 rb-b-332

Gray, William 1835 rb-g-285

Gray, William F. 1834 rb-g-69

Gray, James 1820 rb-c-352

Green, Ann 1820 rb-c-360

Green, Wesley 1835 rb-g-249

Green, Catharine 1845 rb-j-351

Greenfield, William 1835 rb-g-215

Grice, James 1855 rb-o-16

Grice, Lewis 1845 rb-j-467

Griffin, William D. 1846 rb-k-42

Grimes, James 1831 rb-f-182

Grizzard, Joel 1830 rb-f-94

Grizzard, Sally 1836 rb-g-333

Guyan, Patrick 1861 rb-p-595

Hackney, Thomas 1845 rb-j-379

Hackney, Frances 1843 rb-j-46

Hackney, Thomas 1845 rb-j-381

Hagie, Solomon 1845 rb-j-419

Hail, W. 1833 rb-f-510

Halsel, Elizabeth (Mrs.) 1834 rb-g-80

Halsel, Elizabeth 1834 rb-g-27

Halsel, Oney W. 1835 rb-g-81

Halsel, Thomas 1835 rb-g-133

Halsel, Elizabeth 1834 rb-g-30

Halsel, Thomas 1826 rb-d-526

Halsul, J. B. 1846 rb-k-148

Hamelton, Samuel 1847 rb-k-372

Hamilton, James 1854 wb-n-207

Hamilton, Nicholas 1854 wb-n-345

Hamilton, Samuel 1853 wb-n-39

Hamilton, Alexander 1840 rb-h-416

Hamilton, Mary 1845 rb-j-303

Hampton, Abner V. 1823 rb-d-159

Hampton, John 1854 wb-n-251

Hampton, Mary N. 1813 rb-b-156

Hampton, Mary Y.? 1813 rb-b-91

Hampton, Abner V. 1825 rb-d-467

Hancock, Thomas 1817 rb-b-470

Hancock, Thos. G. 1852 wb-m-543

Hancock, Burrel A. 1858 rb-o-765

Hancock, David G. 1855 wb-n-626

Hand, Jane 1814 rb-b-173

Hand, Jean 1814 rb-b-213

Hand, Levy 1813 rb-b-97

Handlin, John 1820 rb-c-355

Hankins, William 1824 rb-d-328

Hansbrough, Marcus 1838 rb-h-126

Hardy, O. 1859 rb-p-57

Hardy, Obadiah 1859 rb-p-69

Harelson, Burgess 1822 rb-d-47

Harelson, Burgess 1833 rb-f-536

Hargrove, Etheldred 1850 wb-m-128

Hargroves, Thomas 1802 rb-a-160

Harmon, Adam 1814 rb-b-187

Harmon, Adam jr. 1814 rb-b-154

Harris, Arthur 1854 wb-n-342

Harris, Augustin 1849 rb-l-228

Harris, Augustus A. 1848 rb-l-100

Harris, Benjamin 1814 rb-b-179

Harris, Ephraim Thomas 1832 rb-f-232

Harris, Harrison H. 1835 rb-g-239

Harris, R. F. 1856 rb-o-101

Harris, R. T. 1855 wb-n-570

Harris, Samuel 1824 rb-d-295

Harris, William 1855 wb-n-491

Harris, Abner 1826 rb-e-1

Harris, Archer 1828 rb-e-275

Harris, Archer 1832 rb-f-408

Harris, Augustus 1848 rb-l-99

Harris, Ransum 1857 rb-o-510

Harrison, Bedee A. 1849 rb-l-259

Harrison, Charles R. 1835 rb-g-104

Harrison, David 1821 rb-c-493

Harrison, David 1831 rb-f-158

Harrison, Joseph 1851 wb-m-222

Harrison, Mary 1838 rb-h-149

Harrison, Mary 1854 wb-n-296

Harrison, Travis 1857 rb-o-359

Harrison, David 1821 rb-c-518

Harrison, David 1822 rb-d-83

Harrison, Mary H. 1829 rb-e-485

Harrison, William 1833 rb-g-442

Harriss, Eiphraim 1831 rb-f-198

Harriss, John 1815 rb-b-79

Harrisson, Mildred 1846 rb-k-50

Hart, William 1853 wb-n-67

Harvey, Berry 1849 rb-l-479

Harvey, Elizabeth 1813 rb-b-144

Harvey, J. B. 1849 rb-l-508

Harvey, James 1815 rb-b-218

Harvey, William 1812 rb-b-60

Harvey, Zachariah 1815 rb-b-283

Harvie, Wm. 1859 rb-p-297

Hatcher, Amos 1836 rb-g-332

Hatcher, John 1850 rb-l-533

Hatcher, Benjaman 1857 rb-o-349

Hatcher, Henry 1830 rb-f-20

Hatcher, Henry 1857 rb-o-470

Hatcher, Polly B. 1846 rb-k-115

Hatcher, R. N. 1860 rb-p-394

Hatsel, John B. 1845 rb-j-426

Hawkins, E. O. 1858 rb-p-15

Hawkins, Joseph J. 1850 wb-m-57

Hawkins, Samuel 1822 rb-d-91

Hawkins, Samuel C. 1829 rb-e-405

Haynes, Anthony 1819 rb-c-213

Haynes, David O. 1844 rb-j-268

Haynes, William 1841 rb-i-58

Haynes, Nancy 1830 rb-f-116

Heathcock, John 1855 wb-n-627

Heathcock, Young 1841 rb-i-116

Heathenan, James sr. 1846 rb-k-308

Heathman, Elizabeth 1859 rb-p-152

Heathman, Elizabethh F. 1861 rb-p-616

Heathman, James 1848 rb-l-195

Heathman, Joseph 1844 rb-j-123

Heathman, James 1832 rb-f-401

Heflin, Absalom 1833 rb-f-510

Heflin, Simon 1861 rb-p-546

Heflin, Susan 1859 rb-p-33

Heggio, Solomon 1845 rb-k-35

Henderson, B. E. 1860 rb-p-410

Henderson, Bennet E. 1860 rb-p-414

Henderson, L. B. 1858 rb-o-789

Henderson, Marrion 1856 rb-o-68

Henderson, Selena B. 1856 rb-o-166

Henderson, Daniel 1836 rb-g-427

Henderson, John 1849 rb-l-422

Hendrick, Jas. 1850 wb-m-52

Henly, Thomas 1860 rb-p-410

Henry, James 1828 rb-e-258

Hensely, Catharine 1830 rb-f-20

Hensley, Cyprus 1825 rb-d-446

Heraldson, Burges 1821 rb-c-402

Herring, Susan 1858 rb-o-780

Herring, Benjamin 1838 rb-h-153

Herring, Benjamin 1860 rb-p-490

Herring, Brite 1828 rb-e-256

Hervey, Zachariah 1815 rb-b-255

Hester, Marion H. 1858 rb-p-15

Hester, Minerva 1859 rb-p-273

Hester, James 1855 wb-n-625

Hester, Robert 1854 wb-n-393

Hester, Robert sr. 1841 rb-i-215

Hewett, Elizabeth 1829 rb-f-3

Heydons, Joseph 1819 rb-c-135

Hibbs, H. W. 1856 rb-o-50

Hibbs, W. W. 1855 wb-n-698

High, John W. 1849 rb-l-449

Hignight, John 1816 rb-b-254

Hill, John 1803 rb-a-193

Hill, John T. 1854 wb-n-248

Hilliard, William 1833 rb-f-427

Hinton, John H. 1843 rb-i-452

Hinton, Kimbrough 1822 rb-d-35

Hitt, Nancy 1858 rb-o-761

Hitt, Burrell G. 1846 rb-k-268

Hodges, Charles 1832 rb-f-369

Hodges, Charles S. 1857 rb-o-514

Hodges, Mack 1860 rb-p-479

Hodges, Olive 1858 rb-o-543

Hodges, Oliver 1857 rb-o-476

Hodges, Olivie 1858 rb-o-705

Hodges, Charles 1832 rb-f-386

Hogan, David 1848 rb-l-176

Hogan, Humphrey 1794 rb-a-36

Hogan, John 1819 rb-c-81

Hogan, William 1835 rb-g-148

Hogan, John 1801 rb-a-137

Hogan, Sarah E. 1859 rb-p-265

Hogan, Wilie 1856 rb-o-126

Hogan, William B. 1835 rb-g-74

Holland, Peggy 1833 rb-f-494

Hollinsworth, John G. 1847 rb-k-511

Hollis, A. 1860 rb-p-470

Holloway, William 1846 rb-k-283

Holt, Chacy 1850 wb-m-36

Holt, Chasey (Sanders) 1849 rb-l-367

Holt, Chasey W. 1848 rb-l-14

Holt, Elizabeth 1847 rb-k-593

Holt, George 1831 rb-f-225

Holt, Hannah 1848 rb-l-12

Holt, Reuben 1856 rb-o-86

Holt, Reuben sr. 1839 rb-h-268

Holt, Robin 1856 rb-o-158

Holt, Wm. 1860 rb-p-480

Hooper, William 1827 rb-e-81

Hopson, Joseph 1831 rb-f-224

Hopson, Joseph 1847 rb-k-564

Hopson, Elizabeth 1820 rb-c-370

Hopson, Elizabeth 1821 rb-c-479

Hopson, George B. 1847 rb-k-423

Hopson, Joseph 1831 rb-f-244

Hopson, Sally Ann 1849 rb-l-356

Hord, Robert 1848 rb-l-13

Horn, Axiom 1848 rb-l-149

Horn, Elizabeth 1856 rb-o-89

Horner, Harriet E. 1849 rb-l-258

Horny, Elizabeth 1858 rb-o-638

Hoskins, Jehu sr. 1841 rb-i-169

House, Isham 1806 rb-a-440

House, James 1797 rb-a-17

House, L. S. 1856 rb-o-38

House, R. M. 1859 rb-p-58

Houston, Shadrack L. 1860 rb-p-385

Howard, James 1855 wb-n-674

Howard, John H. 1830 rb-f-138

Howard, Edward 1854 wb-n-245

Howard, John H. 1830 rb-f-144

Howard, William 1854 wb-n-215

Hubbard, William 1814 rb-b-172

Hudson, John 1826 rb-d-536

Huflen, Absalom 1841 rb-i-115

Humphrey, Charles 1837 rb-g-514

Humphreys, George 1836 rb-g-446

Humphries, Richard 1810 rb-a-486

Hunt, Solomon 1841 rb-i-190

Hunter, E. W. 1850 wb-m-7

Hunter, Lucy 1850 rb-l-625

Hunter, Martin R. 1848 rb-l-44

Hunter, Mathew 1846 rb-k-345

Hunter, Mathew B. 1846 rb-k-282

Hunter, Thomas 1836 rb-g-342

Hunter, Allen 1820 rb-c-366

Hunter, Elizabeth W. 1849 rb-l-498

Hunter, M. R. 1849 rb-l-500

Hunter, Mathew R. 1846 rb-k-251

Hurd, William 1820 rb-c-324

Hurst, Arthur R. 1856 rb-o-276

Hurst, E. (Mrs.) 1859 rb-p-24

Hurst, Elizabeth 1858 rb-o-662

Hurt, Arthur H. 1854 wb-n-208

Husk, Joseph 1812 rb-b-50

Hust, Elizabeth 1860 rb-p-459

Hust, Joseph 1812 rb-b-82

Hust, William 1843 rb-i-528

Hutcher, Henry 1857 rb-o-490

Hutcherson, John T. 1854 wb-n-344

Hutcherson, Joshua P. 1828 rb-e-274

Hutchings, John 1860 rb-p-441

Hutchison, James 1850 wb-m-110

Hutchison, John 1822 rb-d-106

Hutchison, Jas. 1850 wb-m-60

Hutchison, John sr. 1826 rb-d-524

Hutson, John 1821 rb-c-530

Hyde, Alexander F. 1840 rb-i-49

Hyde, Alexander H. 1840 rb-i-4

Ingram, Cythia 1856 rb-o-227

Ingram, Moses 1852 wb-m-602

Ingram, Sterling 1823 rb-d-206

Irvine, James H. 1828 rb-e-376

Irwin, Adaline B. B. 1851 wb-m-217

Irwin, Joseph M. 1849 rb-l-205

Isbell, George 1855 wb-n-685

Isbell, George sr. 1857 rb-o-350

Isbell, George 1855 wb-n-686

Jackson, Brice 1832 rb-f-335

Jackson, Gilliam 1813 rb-b-92

Jackson, J. B. 1861 rb-p-649

Jackson, J. M. 1846 rb-k-329

Jackson, Joe Berry 1861 rb-p-623

Jackson, John 1841 rb-i-95

Jackson, John A. W. 1840 rb-i-6

Jackson, John M. 1847 rb-k-383

Jackson, Joseph 1857 rb-o-493

Jackson, Martha J. 1853 wb-m-633

Jackson, Martha Jane 1856 rb-o-65

Jackson, Archibald 1856 rb-o-219

Jackson, Martha J. 1853 wb-m-640

James, Philip 1813 rb-b-90

James, Philip H. 1813 rb-b-188

Jamison, Wm. C. 1835 rb-g-198

Jamison, Eleanor 1835 rb-g-181

Jamison, William Caldwell 1821 rb-c-532

Jarrell, Wm. 1861 rb-p-623

Jefferis, James 1816 rb-b-335

Jenkins, John 1828 rb-e-363

Jenney, Able 1807 rb-a-462

Jett, Asa H. 1847 rb-k-451

Jett, Edward 1854 wb-n-364

Jett, Edward jr. 1861 rb-p-557

Jett, Edward sr. 1861 rb-p-557

Jinkins, John 1812 rb-a-69

Johnson, A. F. 1861 rb-p-650

Johnson, Abel 1831 rb-f-197

Johnson, Burrel 1860 rb-p-446

Johnson, Elizabeth 1852 wb-m-444

Johnson, Henry 1836 rb-h-172

Johnson, Henry H. 1836 rb-g-338

Johnson, Hinty? 1815 rb-b-286

Johnson, James 1824 rb-d-293

Johnson, John 1815 rb-b-297

Johnson, John A. 1848 rb-l-10

Johnson, John S. 1847 rb-k-567

Johnson, Joseph 1832 rb-f-324

Johnson, Joseph N. 1841 rb-i-189

Johnson, Josiah 1826 rb-d-548

Johnson, Julius 1850 rb-l-588

Johnson, Philip 1822 rb-d-104

Johnson, Susan 1838 rb-h-148

Johnson, Thomas 1848 rb-k-721

Johnson, Abel 1849 rb-l-386

Johnson, Aquilla 1835 rb-g-182

Johnson, Edwin M. 1852 wb-m-459

Johnson, Fauntley 1815 rb-b-148

Johnson, John 1839 rb-h-332

Johnson, Jonathan 1836 rb-g-439

Jones, Abbrigton 1834 rb-f-542

Jones, Albrighton 1837 rb-g-549

Jones, David 1840 rb-h-388

Jones, Ezekial 1850 wb-m-76

Jones, James 1836 rb-g-401

Jones, James S. 1834 rb-g-60*

Jones, Jordan 1840 rb-h-456

Jones, Joshua 1833 rb-f-512

Jones, Nancy 1843 rb-j-57

Jones, Rebecca 1830 rb-f-114

Jones, Reuben 1857 rb-o-396

Jones, Reubin 1827 rb-e-92

Jones, Sarah 1853 wb-n-163

Jones, Stephen G. 1823 rb-d-242

Jones, Thomas 1818 rb-c-19

Jones, Thomas A. 1857 rb-o-472

Jones, Thomas T. 1818 rb-b-510

Jones, W. J. 1856 rb-o-191

Jones, Walter 1854 wb-n-226

Jones, Albrighton 1838 rb-h-33

Jones, Ezekiel 1822 rb-d-8

Jones, Ezekiel 1832 rb-f-332

Jones, Joshua 1834 rb-f-570

Jones, Reuben 1857 rb-o-423

Jones, Thomas 1822 rb-d-37

Jones, Thomas 1828 rb-e-326

Jones, Willie 1838 rb-h-138

Jordan, Benjamin W. 1846 rb-k-49

Jordan, Grizzle 1851 wb-m-374

Jordan, Marcellus 1841 rb-i-186

Jordan, Samuel 1850 wb-m-79

Jordan, G. W. 1851 wb-m-371

Jordan, William 1815 rb-b-165

Joyner, Whitehead 1821 rb-c-440

Kay, Francis 1843 rb-i-519

Keesee, R. C. 1845 rb-j-363

Kelley, Eleanor B. 1848 rb-l-118

Kelsick, Mary 1837 rb-g-606

Kelsick, Will R. 1825 rb-d-498

Kelsick, William 1827 rb-e-132

Kendrick, Dennis L. 1835 rb-g-152

Kendrick, James 1847 rb-k-568

Kendrick, D. D. (D. L.?) 1828 rb-e-396

Kendrick, Dennis L. 1842 rb-i-230

Kerchervall, Sally Ann 1825 rb-d-496

Kerk, Samuel 1828 rb-e-387

Kerr, William 1815 rb-b-277

Kesee, Rewben 1844 rb-j-266

Ketrell, Salomon 1830 rb-f-121

Ketsick, William R. 1828 rb-e-285

Kettrell, Soloman A. 1818 rb-b-389

Killebrew, Buckner 1846 rb-k-191

Killebrew, Edithy O. 1854 wb-n-209

Killebrew, Eliza 1849 rb-l-384

Killebrew, Eliza Jane 1851 wb-m-329

Killebrew, Glidewell 1829 rb-e-491

Killebrew, Margaret 1856 rb-o-193

Killebrew, Margaret Ann 1856 rb-o-228

Killebrew, Whitfield 1859 rb-p-120

Killebrew, Buckner 1824 rb-d-372

Killebrew, Buckner 1846 rb-k-77

Killebrew, Edwin 1847 rb-k-669

King, Alexander 1844 rb-j-84

King, H. R. 1840 rb-i-44

King, H. R. jr. 1849 rb-l-391

King, Holcom R. 1849 rb-l-351

King, Holcomb 1840 rb-i-23

King, John 1825 rb-d-419

King, M. M. (Mrs.) 1860 rb-p-512

King, Madison 1835 rb-g-214

King, Thomas 1831 rb-f-196

King, Thomas A. 1858 rb-o-614

King, W. 1836 rb-g-301

King, William 1810 rb-a-357

King, Benjamin 1847 rb-k-457

King, John 1805 rb-a-309

King, W. B. 1852 wb-m-565

Kirchevall, Sally Ann 1845 rb-j-345

Kirk, Samuel 1827 rb-e-54

Kittrell, Isaac 1811 rb-b-12

Kittrell, James 1811 rb-b-25

Knott, John W. 1853 wb-n-166

Knox, Joseph C. 1846 rb-k-256

Knox, J. C. 1847 rb-k-600

Kussee, R. C. 1847 rb-k-532

Kyle, Daniel 1839 rb-h-296

Lamb, Meablen? E. 1858 rb-o-602

Lamb, John 1851 wb-m-270

Lambeth, Susan 1840 rb-h-439

Lambeth, Thomas 1837 rb-h-21

Langston, William 1855 wb-n-605

Lankford, Nicholas 1848 rb-l-94

Lankford, Hiram 1844 rb-j-288

Layne, Ann Z. 1850 rb-l-616

Layne, John 1840 rb-h-455

Lee, Benjamin D. 1837 rb-g-625

Lee, Robert L. 1842 rb-i-266

Lee, Robert S. 1844 rb-j-164

Lee, Shaderick 1842 rb-i-443

Lee, Charles W. 1820 rb-c-338

Lee, Mary 1859 rb-p-143

Lee, Richard 1814 rb-b-192

Lee, Washington 1835 rb-g-138

Lefland, James S. 1855 wb-n-645

Leggett, Henry R. 1850 rb-l-592

Leigh, Mary 1857 rb-o-482

Leigh, Polly (Mary) 1860 rb-p-310

Leigh, Polly 1857 rb-o-445

Leigh, Rachael 1827 rb-e-64

Leigh, Richard 1828 rb-e-345

Leigh, Washington 1826 rb-e-40

Leigh, Richard 1829 rb-e-509

Ligon, Lucy R. 1840 rb-h-449

Ligon, Nicholas P. 1834 rb-f-545

Ligon, Joseph 1825 rb-d-433

Ligon, Joseph 1842 rb-i-414

Ligon, Matthew 1843 rb-i-480

Linzy, Abigal 1801? rb-a-160

Little, Elizabeth 1858 rb-o-714

Little, Henry 1849 rb-l-305

Lizenby, Henry 1838 rb-h-120

Lockert, Moses 1818 rb-c-21

Lofland, James L. 1857 rb-o-287

Lofland, James S. 1856 rb-o-46

Loggins, William 1817 rb-b-419

Long, Andrew 1861 rb-p-559

Long, William 1828 rb-e-370

Loughran, Sylvania H. 1843 rb-j-25

Love, David 1830 rb-f-134

Lowther, William Lewis 1821 rb-d-3

Lowther, John W. 1810 rb-a-349

Lyal, Catharine 1835 rb-g-156

Lyal, Robert M. 1832 rb-f-396

Lyle, James L. 1859 rb-p-278

Lyle, Thomas 1850 wb-m-4

Lyle, J. L. 1859 rb-p-265

Lyle, Jordan 1843 rb-i-505

Lyle, Thomas 1850 rb-l-621

Lyles, John 1821 rb-c-506

Lynch, David 1850 rb-l-624

Lynch, David 1850 rb-l-631

Lynes, William J. 1833 rb-f-475

Lynes, Samuel 1841 rb-i-194

Lynus, Violetta S. 1859 rb-p-33

Lyon, Nicholas P. 1837 rb-g-547

Lyon, Elly 1831 rb-f-239

Lyons, Ameline 1859 rb-p-119

Lyons, Guthridge 1827 rb-e-84

Lyson, Uriah 1850 rb-l-513

Mackey, John 1821 rb-c-459

Malam?, Susanna Ann 1855 wb-n-646

Mallory, Francis 1823 rb-d-111

Mallory, George 1823 rb-d-241

Mallory, George S. 1823 rb-d-272

Mallory, Stephen 1835 rb-g-225

Mallory, Stephen 1846 rb-k-292

Mallory, Thomas 1814 rb-b-201

Mallory, Thomas 1832 rb-f-387

Mallory, Frances 1832 rb-f-464

Mallory, James 1833 rb-f-463

Mallory, Stephen 1836 rb-g-265

Malone, Fred 1860 rb-p-510

Manafee, J. M. 1854 wb-n-319

Manley, Nicholas 1857 rb-o-491

Manson, Thomas 1855 wb-n-687

Manson, Thomas H. 1857 rb-o-408

Marable, J. H. 1844 rb-j-217

Marable, John H. sr. 1844 rb-j-142

Marable, Mary M. 1843 rb-i-467

Marable, Ann J. 1860 rb-p-313

Marlin, John 1841 rb-i-138

Marr, Ann G. 1847 rb-k-371

Marr, C. H. P. 1854 wb-n-340

Marrow, James H. 1846 rb-k-352

Marsh, A. O. 1860 rb-p-470

Marshall, John 1838 rb-h-122

Marshall, Carter 1823 rb-d-253

Martin, Alexander T. 1851 wb-m-272

Martin, Ambrose 1851 wb-m-174

Martin, Ambrose jr. 1847 rb-k-625

Martin, Bradley 1857 rb-o-415

Martin, John 1840 rb-i-33

Martin, M. A. 1851 wb-m-328

Martin, Susan C. 1844 rb-j-265

Martin, William E. 1844 rb-j-167

Martin, Jesse 1820 rb-c-323

Martin, M. N. 1856 rb-o-113

Martin, William E. 1834 rb-g-39

Mason, John 1827 rb-e-174

Mathes, Thomas 1847 rb-k-493

Mathews, Drury 1847 rb-k-664

Mathis, William 1826 rb-d-544

McAlister, John 1820 rb-c-301

McAlister, Marcus 1834 rb-g-56

McAlister, John 1826 rb-e-33

McAllister, John 1827 rb-e-195

McBee, Risden H. 1851 wb-m-304

McBride, A. 1854 wb-n-317

McBride, Alfred 1854 wb-n-374

McCallester, John jr. 1820 rb-c-293

McCaucle?, Mary C. 1860 rb-p-479

McCaughan, James 1842 rb-i-316

McCauley, John 1843 rb-i-499

McCauley, William 1822 rb-d-107

McCauley, George 1860 rb-p-442

McCauley, John sr. 1842 rb-i-362

McCauley, John sr. 1842 rb-i-405

McClure, Hugh 1839 rb-h-269

McClure, James B. 1838 rb-h-30

McClure, James B. 1851 wb-m-282

McClure, William 1831 rb-f-226

McClure, Hugh 1828 rb-e-260

McClure, James 1849 rb-l-302

McClure, Thomas 1845 rb-j-352

McClure, William 1831 rb-f-238

McClurey, W. A. 1860 rb-p-471

McCool, James 1856 rb-o-258

McCorkle, Joseph 1803 rb-a-181

McCormick, Thomas 1815 rb-b-260

McCrabb, Alexander 1811 rb-b-14

McCutchen, John 1833 rb-f-534

McCutchen, Valentine 1815 rb-b-293

McCutchin, Valentine 1830 rb-f-30

McCuthin, John 1833 rb-f-473

McDaniel, Harriette E. 1839 rb-h-296

McDaniel, Johnson 1806 rb-a-440

McDaniel, George 1855 wb-n-683

McDougle, Thomas 1850 rb-l-629

McDougle, Thomas 1850 rb-l-630

McFadden, A. V. 1853 wb-m-648

McFadden, D. 1834 rb-g-22

McFadden, David sr. 1838 rb-h-42

McFadden, Jame 1857 rb-o-513

McFaddin, Andrew 1853 wb-n-24

McFaddin, David 1834 rb-g-77

McFaddin, David 1851 wb-m-255

McFaddin, David jr. 1836 rb-g-402

McFaddin, John 1848 rb-k-718

McFaddin, Mary 1848 rb-l-154

McFaddin, David 1835 rb-g-221

McFall, Henry 1850 wb-m-15

McFall, Sally A. S. 1852 wb-m-619

McFall, Sally Ann S. 1855 wb-n-671

McFall, Samuel 1859 rb-p-260

McFall, Zany 1852 wb-m-620

McFarland, James 1797 rb-b-70

McGehee, Thomas 1834 rb-f-614

McGehee, Thomas jr. 1836 rb-g-427

McGowen, Robert 1820 rb-c-269

McGuire, Francis 1848 rb-k-748

McGuire, John 1835 rb-g-245

McGuire, John 1835 rb-g-108

McIntyre, Charles 1855 wb-n-690

McKennie, William 1816 rb-b-363

McLean, Marcia F. 1821 rb-c-494

McManis, David 1845 rb-j-417

McMordie, Robert 1859 rb-p-278

McNichols, Samuel 1846 rb-k-142

Meacham, J. B. 1856 rb-o-92

Meacham, James 1846 rb-k-275

Meacham, John 1860 rb-p-407

Meacham, John S. 1860 rb-p-386

Meacham, John L. 1859 rb-p-284

Meanley, William 1823 rb-d-188

Meatcham, Spencer 1835 rb-g-284

Medlock, Elizabeth 1827 rb-e-94

Mellon, Thomas 1842 rb-i-267

Melton, Patterson 1820 rb-c-391

Menefee, James N. 1854 wb-n-412

Menifee, John N. 1858 rb-o-672

Mereck, Richard 1803 rb-a-184

Meriwether, Charles 1815 rb-b-72

Merritt, R. A. 1861 rb-p-614

Mewell, John 1821 rb-c-499

Michem, Spencer 1835 rb-g-190

Mickle, John C. 1859 rb-p-208

Mickle, George 1842 rb-k-40

Mickle, John C. 1859 rb-p-233

Miller, Elizabeth 1821 rb-c-427

Miller, Ralph 1814 rb-b-189

Miller, John C. 1839 rb-h-311

Miller, Ralph 1801 rb-a-131

Minor, Charles 1842 rb-i-442

Minor, John 1817 rb-b-421

Minor, Mary Ann 1835 rb-g-253

Minor, Thomas O. 1819 rb-g-87

Minor, John 1822 rb-d-66

Minor, Thomas C. 1824 rb-d-391

Minor, Thomas Carr 1819 rb-c-130

Minton?, R. D. 1855 wb-n-551

Mirick, Richard 1802 rb-a-162

Mirick, Richard 1826 rb-e-39

Mitchel, Daniel 1825 rb-d-500

Mitchel, Mesnier 1823 rb-d-211

Mitchell, David 1830 rb-f-100

Mitchell, Delphia 1821 rb-c-421

Mitchell, James 1857 rb-o-418

Mitchell, William H. 1837 rb-g-489

Mitchell, William S. 1819 rb-c-75

Mitchell, Daniel 1830 rb-f-104

Mitchell, James 1857 rb-o-422

Mitchell, Misenier 1823 rb-d-227

Mitchell, William S. 1822 rb-d-86

Mockbee, Ann S. 1840 rb-h-462

Mockbee, John 1836 rb-g-289

Mockbee, Mary C. 1859 rb-p-19

Monroe, William 1842 rb-i-428

Moody, Elizabeth 1857 rb-o-375

Moody, James 1846 rb-k-9

Moody, James W. 1845 rb-k-131

Moody, Theodrick 1853 wb-n-69

Moore (B), Ben 1853 wb-n-173

Moore, Ben 1853 wb-n-304

Moore, Daniel 1857 rb-o-512

Moore, David 1857 rb-o-531

Moore, George H. 1857 rb-o-396

Moore, Horace G. 1851 wb-m-324

Moore, Lewis 1832 rb-f-417

Moore, Mary 1849 rb-l-456

Moore, R. S. 1861 rb-p-592

Moore, Thomas 1836 rb-g-462

Moore, Thomas S. 1836 rb-g-429

Moore, William 1813 rb-b-133

Moore, George H. 1857 rb-o-424

Moore, Gully 1825 rb-e-86

Moorehouse, J. B. 1857 rb-o-327

More, Lewis 1819 rb-c-207

Morgan, Francis N. 1829 rb-f-5

Morgan, James T. 1860 rb-p-385

Morgan, Willis Montgomery 1860 rb-p-330

Morgan, Willis sr. 1860 rb-p-410

Morgan, Willis 1857 rb-o-526

Morris, Adley 1811 rb-b-11

Morris, Aquilla 1827 rb-e-91

Morris, Charles P. 1861 rb-p-545

Morris, John T. 1859 rb-p-57

Morris, Nathan D. 1852 wb-m-443

Morris, Thomas 1822 rb-d-20

Morris, Will 1837 rb-h-18

Morris, William 1853 wb-n-175

Morris, William M. 1857 rb-o-430

Morris, Wm. sr. 1835 rb-g-243

Morris, Nathan 1830 rb-f-65

Morrison, Asahel 1832 rb-f-312

Morrison, Daniel 1853 wb-n-161

Morrison, James 1831 rb-f-300

Morrison, James 1856 rb-o-262

Morrison, William 1812 rb-b-37

Morrison, Daniel 1853 wb-n-162

Morrow, James H. 1843 rb-j-48

Morrow, Louisa 1861 rb-p-579

Morrow, N. B. 1861 rb-p-642

Morrow, Susan Ann 1855 wb-n-704

Morrow, William 1846 rb-k-684

Morrow, James 1845 rb-j-394

Morrow, Lovicie 1859 rb-p-283

Morrow, Sarah 1845 rb-j-394

Moseley, H. W. 1856 rb-o-220

Moseley, Jesse 1817 rb-b-399

Moseley, John S. 1844 rb-j-261

Mosely, Edward 1841 rb-i-195

Mosely, H. H. 1856 rb-o-91

Mosely, Thomas 1819 rb-c-179

Mosely, John 1836 rb-g-452

Mosely, John 1853 wb-m-634

Mosley, John S. 1844 rb-j-125

Moss, J. P. 1856 rb-o-137

Moss, John D. 1854 wb-n-394

Mullins, Sarah 1849 rb-l-503

Mumford, M. B. 1850 wb-m-148

Mumford, Marshall 1848 rb-l-133

Mumford, W. B. 1859 rb-p-200

Murdy, Stephen 1843 rb-i-536

Murison, James 1830 rb-f-92

Murphee, Mathew 1803 rb-a-174

Murphy, Jenkins 1847 rb-k-575

Murphy, Patrick 1800 rb-a-119

Murphy, W. B. 1847 rb-k-592

Murphy, Jenkins 1848 rb-k-484

Murphy, Warren B. 1847 rb-k-636

Myers, Martha A. 1860 rb-p-386

Nanny, Abel 1844 rb-j-250

Napier, Mary 1821 rb-c-474

Neblet, John sr. 1830 rb-f-115

Neblet, Josiah D. 1854 wb-n-442

Neblett, E. C. 1850 wb-m-127

Neblett, Francis 1820 rb-c-346

Neblett, John 1837 rb-g-522

Neblett, Josiah (Doctor) 1842 rb-i-447

Neblett, Josiah D. 1848 rb-l-117

Neblett, R. A. 1859 rb-p-296

Neblett, Sally 1848 rb-k-716

Neblett, Stephen 1845 rb-j-416

Neblett, Sterling 1845 rb-j-326

Neblett, Susanna 1837 rb-g-635

Neblett, William 1851 wb-m-317

Neblett, Edward 1845 rb-k-1

Neblett, Elizabeth N. 1858 rb-o-716

Neblett, John sr. 1830 rb-f-117

Neblett, Josiah 1842 rb-i-393

Neblett, Sterling sr. 1844 rb-j-272

Neely, Wm. 1833 rb-f-428

Nelson, George B. 1838 rb-h-42

Nelson, M. A. 1839 rb-h-196

Nelson, Robert 1808 rb-a-341

Nelson, Robert 1818 rb-c-55

Nelson, William 1820 rb-c-284

Nelson, William 1830 rb-f-138

Nevell, Rachael 1845 rb-j-299

Nevil, Rachel 1829 rb-e-492

Nevill, George 1811 rb-a-56

Neville, George 1821 rb-c-403

Neville, Mary 1843 rb-j-18

Neville, John 1853 wb-n-189

Newbury, James 1832 rb-f-366

Newel, Edward 1843 rb-j-23

Newell, John 1818 rb-c-52

Newell, S. S. 1852 wb-m-430

Newell, William 1844 rb-j-285

Newsom, Gilliam 1829 rb-e-494

Newton, Richard D. 1851 wb-m-273

Niblet, John sr. 1832 rb-f-382

Niblet?, Jane 1855 wb-n-635

Niblett, Jane R. 1853 wb-n-1

Niblett, William 1853 wb-n-134

Niblett, Elija H. 1855 wb-n-635

Nicholson, Brittian 1833 rb-f-486

Nicholson, Griffin 1849 rb-l-483

Nicholson, B. 1833 rb-f-494

Nicholson, Griffin 1828 rb-e-340

Nicholson, Mary 1844 rb-j-64

Nolen, Alen 1814 rb-b-162

Nolen, Thomas 1851 wb-m-192

Norfleet, Cordall 1834 rb-g-153

Norfleet, James B. 1839 rb-h-254

Norfleet, James sr. 1839 rb-h-214

Norfleet, Thomas J. 1837 rb-h-29

Northington, E. C. (Miss) 1860 rb-p-516

Northington, E. N. 1856 rb-o-127

Northington, Felix G. 1859 rb-p-171

Northington, Felix jr. 1856 rb-o-126

Northington, John 1836 rb-g-263

Northington, Samuel 1844 rb-j-61

Norwood, Elizabeth P. 1841 rb-i-120

Nuell, S. S. 1854 wb-n-331

Nuell, William 1846 rb-k-360

Nurrel, Edward 1845 rb-k-21

Nurrel, Wm. 1845 rb-k-76

Obarr, Daniel 1819 rb-c-80

Odeneal, Tate (Lt.) 1816 rb-b-57

Odeneal, Tate 1816 rb-b-311

Ogburn, James M. 1858 rb-o-674

Ogburn, Josiah 1829 rb-f-1

Ogburn, Sarah 1824 rb-d-299

Ogburn, Sarah 1846 rb-k-52

Ogburn, John 1854 wb-n-379

Ogburn, Matthew 1839 rb-h-359

Ogburn, Sarah 1824 rb-d-301

Ogg, Elizabeth 1861 rb-p-559

Ogg, Wm. 1860 rb-p-409

Oldham, Jessee 1845 rb-j-318

Oldham, Joel R. 1810 rb-a-413

Oldham, Moses 1819 rb-c-85

Oldham, Moses 1860 rb-p-471

Oldham, Moses sr. 1818 rb-b-489

Oldham, George 1829 rb-e-535

Oldham, James K. 1860 rb-p-518

Oldham, Jessee 1840 rb-h-374

Oneal, Peter 1845 rb-k-38

Orgain, James 1833 rb-f-510

Orgain, Susannah 1840 rb-h-466

Orgain, William D. 1840 rb-i-3

Orgain, Benjamin 1839 rb-h-351

Orgain, Benjamin 1841 rb-i-65

Organ, Upton 1838 rb-h-141

Orr, H. B. 1859 rb-p-200

Osburn, John B. 1852 wb-m-510

Outlaw, George 1843 rb-i-486

Outlaw, George sr. 1842 rb-i-240

Outlaw, J. A. 1846 rb-k-272

Outlaw, John A. 1846 rb-k-317

Outlaw, John A. jr. 1850 rb-l-602

Outlaw, Thomas 1849 rb-l-380

Outlaw, Thomas B. 1847 rb-k-420

Outlaw, Davis 1809 rb-a-143

Outlaw, Wright 1813 rb-b-134

Overton, Richard 1827 rb-e-175

Overton, Richard jr. 1832 rb-f-338

Overton, Richard sr. 1834 rb-f-572

Owen, Christopher 1840 rb-h-415

Owens, Christopher 1828 rb-e-203

Owens, Sophia 1838 rb-h-94

Pace, William 1845 rb-j-453

Pain, Cyntha Ann 1857 rb-o-352

Paine, John T. 1855 wb-n-615

Paine, Mary A. J. 1846 rb-k-82

Paine, Thomas 1846 rb-k-330

Paine, Harriet 1858 rb-o-584

Paine, James 1818 rb-d-90

Paine, James E. 1852 wb-m-606

Paine, John L. 1853 wb-n-89

Pardue, Richard 1810 rb-a-396

Parham, Charles S. 1859 rb-p-209

Parham, Charles L? 1859 rb-p-220

Parker, Dolly 1837 rb-g-518

Parker, J. W. 1848 rb-l-202

Parker, Jehu 1838 rb-h-95

Parker, John 1841 rb-i-224

Parker, Priscilla 1846 rb-k-259

Parker, T. W. 1848 rb-l-163

Parker, Thomas 1819 rb-c-214

Parrish, Benjamin 1848 rb-k-720

Parrish, George H. 1834 rb-g-23

Payne, Harriet E. 1860 rb-p-405

Payne, Samuel D. 1861 rb-p-568

Peay, Austin 1853 wb-n-63

Peay, William 1831 rb-f-195

Peck, Francis 1859 rb-p-209

Peeples, Agathy 1817 rb-b-449

Peeples, Burrell H. 1819 rb-c-134

Peeples, David 1816 rb-b-374

Peeples, Nathan 1820 rb-c-359

Pegram, Benjamin 1832 rb-f-494

Pennington, Isaac 1801 rb-a-143

Pennington, John 1797 rb-a-19

Penrice, Joseph 1812 rb-b-41

Penrice, Sally 1826 rb-d-529

Perrington, Elizabeth J. 1848 rb-k-690

Perrington, T. A. U. 1852 wb-m-596

Perrington, Thomas A. 1850 wb-m-103

Perry, A. H. 1854 wb-n-448

Perry, William 1807 rb-a-445

Perry, Josiah 1832 rb-f-4001

Persney, B. P. 1861 rb-p-527

Person, B. P. 1861 rb-p-549

Peterson, Rowland 1836 rb-g-290

Pettus, Thomas B. 1851 wb-m-389

Philips, David 1803 rb-a-171

Philips, Eliza 1853 wb-n-75

Phillips, Eliza G. 1849 rb-l-352

Phillips, Johnathan 1839 rb-h-194

Pickering, Spencer 1846 rb-k-288

Picket, Charles 1807 rb-a-49

Poindexter, Andrew B. 1855 wb-n-566

Poindexter, Lewis T. 1859 rb-p-245

Pollard, G. M. 1858 rb-o-606

Pollard, Rebecca 1855 wb-n-697

Pollard, John E. 1852 wb-m-520

Pollard, Margaret 1847 rb-k-614

Pollard, Reuben 1851 wb-m-343

Pollard, Reubin 1843 rb-j-38

Pool, Lucretia 1847 rb-k-396

Pool, John 1859 rb-p-95

Poor, Elizabeth 1835 rb-g-229

Poor, Sarah E. 1835 rb-g-254

Porter, Mary 1834 rb-f-615

Porter, Thomas 1815 rb-b-314

Porter, Thomas S. 1816 rb-b-251

Poston, John H. 1848 rb-l-146

Potter, Thomas 1817 rb-b-420

Potter, Thomas S. 1815 rb-b-282

Powell, Hampton 1852 wb-m-431

Powell, James 1841 rb-i-193

Power, Samuel D. 1832 rb-f-346

Powers, R. C. 1860 rb-p-479

Powers, Travis 1854 wb-n-365

Prewen, William 1836 rb-g-272

Price, Sara Ann 1847 rb-k-606

Prichard, John 1821 rb-d-356

Prichard, David 1824 rb-d-370

Priestley, Matilda 1850 wb-m-77

Prince, Robert 1813 rb-a-489

Pritchard, David 1824 rb-d-398

Pritchet, John 1847 rb-k-573

Pritchet, Nancy 1813 rb-b-150

Pritchett, William C. 1830 rb-f-137

Proudfit, John H. 1840 rb-i-9

Proudfoot, Nancy 1855 wb-n-524

Purdue, Orren 1811 rb-b-22

Purrington, T. A. 1851 wb-m-279

Quarles, Garret M. 1847 rb-k-391

Quinn, Lot? 1855 wb-n-597

Radford, Ann (Mrs) 1826 rb-d-551

Radford, Nancy 1824 rb-d-301

Raebourn, Thomas 1799 rb-a-37

Raimy, John R. 1847 rb-k-396

Rainey, Jane 1860 rb-p-513

Ramey, Margaret 1853 wb-n-201

Ramey, Randolph 1841 rb-i-119

Randle, T. S. 1858 rb-p-13

Randle, Thomas W. 1858 rb-o-606

Ransdale, James P. 1839 rb-h-267

Rasford, Nancy 1824 rb-d-297

Rawlings, Alexander H. (Dr.) 1828 rb-e-343

Rawlings, Alexander 1828 rb-e-260

Ray, Nathan 1807 rb-a-333

Read, Mordecai 1828 rb-e-391

Read, Jane 1847 rb-k-562

Reasons, Alfred B. 1834 rb-f-540

Reasons, Alfred P. 1834 rb-f-584

Reasons, Charlotte 1849 rb-l-427

Reasons, Joseph 1840 rb-h-476

Reasons, Sarah 1840 rb-h-434

Reasons, William 1825 rb-d-449

Reasons, William 1840 rb-h-385

Reasons, James 1846 rb-k-110

Reasons, John 1828 rb-e-204

Reasons, William 1825 rb-d-468

Reaves, B. H. 1851 wb-m-314

Reaves, Benjamin 1849 rb-l-353

Redd, Mordecai 1826 rb-e-5

Reed, David 1818 rb-c-57

Reed, Moses 1854 wb-n-318

Reeves, Stephen 1852 wb-m-457

Reves, Charlotte 1849 rb-l-359

Reynolds, James B. 1851 wb-m-326

Reynolds, Susan 1861 rb-p-628

Richardson, Isham 1829 rb-e-514

Richardson, Isham P. 1837 rb-g-624

Ricks, P. W. 1860 rb-p-427

Ridsdale, Jno. 1823 rb-d-273

Riggins, Ruth 1841 rb-i-63

Riggs, James 1826 rb-d-524

Rinehart, Jacob 1854 wb-n-299

Rineheart, John 1855 wb-n-697

Rineheart, Sarah 1860 rb-p-446

Rivers, Mildred 1832 rb-f-368

Rivers, Thomas 1827 rb-e-173

Rives, Stephen 1836 rb-g-264

Rives, Stephen 1849 rb-l-458

Roach, E. B. 1847 rb-k-583

Robbins, John G. 1821 rb-c-405

Robert, Peter P. 1833 rb-f-474

Roberts, Bede 1834 rb-g-26

Roberts, Bedee (Mrs.) 1835 rb-g-191

Roberts, Collin 1812 rb-a-75

Roberts, Peter P. 1833 rb-f-490

Roberts, Samuel 1856 rb-o-67

Roberts, Peter P. 1834 rb-f-603

Roberts, Samuel 1823 rb-d-89

Robertson, S. G. 1853 wb-n-67

Roche, Edward B. 1844 rb-j-256

Rogers, A. M. 1859 rb-p-297

Rogers, A. W. (Dr.) 1861 rb-p-591

Rogers, Armstead 1847 rb-k-615

Rogers, Armsted sr. 1835 rb-g-247

Rogers, Isaac 1824 rb-d-316

Rogers, James 1825 rb-d-472

Rogers, Martha 1825 rb-d-473

Rogers, Wm. 1860 rb-p-423

Rogers, Armstead 1836 rb-g-267

Rogers, Isaac 1814 rb-b-147

Rogers, Isaac 1824 rb-d-413

Rogers, Martha 1825 rb-d-479

Rogers, W. J. 1860 rb-p-393

Rook, Daniel 1837 rb-g-494

Rook, John 1826 rb-e-48

Rook, John sr. 1824 rb-d-385

Rook, Susanna 1826 rb-e-4

Rook, Daniel 1824 rb-d-330

Rook, John sr. 1825 rb-d-435

Rose, Virginia 1856 rb-o-226

Rose, Wiley 1844 rb-j-267

Rose, Wm. 1861 rb-p-574

Rosson, William 1858 rb-o-569

Rowan, Daniel 1801 rb-a-123

Rowley, M. 1842 rb-i-444

Royster, N. M. 1855 wb-n-511

Royster, Nathaniel M. 1838 rb-h-138

Rucker, Thomas D. 1853 wb-n-44

Rudolph, Fredrick 1860 rb-p-445

Rudolph, Thomas S. 1856 rb-o-247

Rudolph, Jacob 1838 rb-h-192

Rudolph, John 1845 rb-k-299

Rush, William 1857 rb-o-505

Russel, John 1825 rb-d-503

Russell, John 1825 rb-d-497

Ryan, James 1850 wb-m-122

Rybourn, Washington 1803 rb-a-172

Rye, Absolam 1823 rb-d-485

Rye, Francis 1847 rb-k-638

Rye, Benjamin 1859 rb-p-283

Rys, Benjamin 1823 rb-d-243

Sale, James H. 1855 wb-n-619

Sale, James H. 1855 wb-n-622

Sallee, William 1857 rb-o-342

Sallee, Wm. F. 1855 wb-n-525

Saller, Widon H. 1855 wb-n-502

Samuel, Edwin 1834 rb-g-64

Samuel, Edwin G. 1836 rb-g-395

Sanderson, Benjamin 1813 rb-b-93

Sanderson, Jesse 1813 rb-b-94

Sanderson, Robert 1814 rb-b-220

Sanderson, Thomas 1815 rb-b-302

Sawyer, Rebecca 1851 wb-m-351

Sawyer, John 1854 wb-n-414

Sawyers, Robert 1840 rb-h-377

Scott, Ellen Lucy 1850 wb-m-56

Scott, Soloman 1807 rb-a-463

Scott, Elizabeth 1859 rb-p-223

Searcy, Bennet 1818 rb-b-508

Sears, Andrew 1842 rb-i-392

Sevier, Valentine 1800 rb-a-114

Shamwell, Joseph 1838 rb-k-774

Shamwell, Marion 1858 rb-o-780

Sharp, Mary 1831 rb-f-259

Shaw, Henry 1819 rb-c-206

Shearron, Thomas 1854 wb-n-250

Shelby, Even 1795 rb-a-5

Shelby, Hargey 1835 rb-g-237

Shelby, Harry 1843 rb-i-511

Shelby, Harvey 1837 rb-g-546

Shelby, Isaac 1835 rb-g-235

Shelby, Jenkin W. 1846 rb-k-119

Shelby, Sally 1821 rb-c-472

Shelby, Thomas 1816 rb-b-376

Shelby, Thomas P. 1817 rb-b-403

Shelby, Isaac 1813 rb-a-503

Shelby, John 1818 rb-b-384

Shelby, John 1823 rb-d-151

Shelbys, Evan jr. 1806 rb-a-260

Shelly, Sally 1821 rb-c-400

Shelton, John 1839 rb-h-325

Shemwell, Joseph 1838 rb-h-87

Shepherd, James 1835 rb-g-230

Shepherd, Frances 1853 wb-m-649

Shepherd, Samuel 1838 rb-h-64

Sherman, Elizabeth 1842 rb-i-227

Sherman, Edmond 1846 rb-k-369

Sherman, Thomas M. 1849 rb-l-500

Short, Joshua 1811 rb-b-23

Shuff, James 1858 rb-o-601

Silcox, James 1818 rb-b-517

Simpson, E. M. 1855 wb-n-595

Sims, Gorge 1805 rb-a-244

Sitcoks?, James 1817 rb-b-397

Skinner, James J. 1850 wb-m-104

Skinner, Leah (Mrs.) 1851 wb-m-279

Skinner, Leah (or Leor) Mrs. 1851 wb-m-248

Skinner, Josiah 1842 rb-i-265

Sloane, David 1802 rb-a-153

Sly, Jacob 1826 rb-d-550

Small, A. L. 1858 rb-o-782

Small, Lewis 1858 rb-o-605

Smith, E. B. 1855 wb-n-631

Smith, Elisha D. 1852 wb-m-603

Smith, Fielding 1826 rb-d-546

Smith, George W. 1848 rb-k-747

Smith, Howell 1820 rb-c-266

Smith, J. A. 1835 rb-g-204

Smith, James 1842 rb-i-434

Smith, John 1813 rb-b-95

Smith, John 1835 rb-g-106

Smith, John A. 1835 rb-g-66

Smith, Levi 1819 rb-c-140

Smith, Polly 1815 rb-b-68

Smith, R. W. 1852 wb-m-437

Smith, Reuben M. 1853 wb-n-62

Smith, Robert 1859 rb-p-298

Smith, Robert W. 1851 wb-m-327

Smith, Thomas 1830 rb-f-137

Smith, Thomas 1840 rb-h-438

Smith, Thomas W. 1844 rb-j-208

Smith, Thos. N. 1836 rb-g-404

Smith, William 1853 wb-n-65

Smith, Lucy 1849 rb-l-406

Smith, Nancy 1851 wb-m-245

Smith, Samuel 1837 rb-g-519

Smith, Samuel 1842 rb-i-376

Smith, Sidney 1843 rb-j-46

Smithwick, Shade 1839 rb-h-263

Smithwick, Slade 1836 rb-g-454

Smoot, W. J. 1846 rb-k-269

Snell, John 1849 rb-l-332

Snell, Lewis 1860 rb-p-435

Snider, Charles 1796 rb-a-13

Sproule, Robert 1827 rb-e-55

St Johns, Elizabeth 1843 rb-j-41

Stack, Adam 1849 wb-m-578

Staily, Fredrick 1815 rb-b-272

Staley, Frederick 1825 rb-d-485

Stamper, Blount 1857 rb-o-288

Stamper, Nicholas 1858 rb-o-704

Stamper, Robert 1832 rb-f-369

Stankey, Abram 1854 wb-n-346

Starkie, Abraham 1846 rb-k-273

Starkie, Pleasant 1835 rb-g-213

Steel, John 1848 rb-l-173

Steele, Edward H. 1828 rb-e-330

Steele, John 1822 rb-d-14

Steele, John sr. 1822 rb-d-84

Steele, Sally 1843 rb-i-510

Stegar, William 1830 rb-f-116

Stephens, Squire 1820 rb-c-302

Stewart, Charles 1817 rb-b-450

Stewart, Duncan 1810 rb-a-510

Stewart, Robert W. 1820 rb-c-356

Stewart, William 1860 rb-p-514

Stewart, James 1810 rb-a-511

Stewart, James 1818 rb-c-62

Stewart, William 1848 rb-l-171

Stone, Robert B. 1837 rb-g-636

Stroud, Joseph 1841 rb-i-106

Stuart, John 1822 rb-d-252

Sturdivant, Joseph 1853 wb-n-123

Sugg, Lemuel 1809 rb-a-452

Syke, Sanford 1832 rb-f-308

Sykes, Jacob 1822 rb-d-20

Sykes, Lunsford 1832 rb-f-348

Tally, Guilford 1859 rb-p-67

Tarrant, Samuel 1797 rb-a-14

Tatom, John 1831 rb-f-311

Tatom, John M. 1831 rb-f-258

Taylor, T. C. 1859 rb-p-111

Taylor, Thomas C. 1859 rb-p-152

Taylor, William 1847 rb-k-619

Taylor, Betsy 1833 rb-f-503

Taylor, Bitcy 1834 rb-f-576

Taylor, E. M. O. 1849 rb-k-767

Taylor, Edmond 1826 rb-e-2

Taylor, Esther (Cooper) 1825 rb-d-517

Taylor, Henry C. 1831 rb-f-202

Taylor, Robert P. 1849 rb-l-454

Taylor, Samuel 1814 rb-b-191

Teas, Charles 1801 rb-a-118

Teasley, John 1816 rb-b-328

Teasley, John 1852 wb-m-608

Teasley, Lucy 1846 rb-k-301

Temple, Francis B. 1838 rb-h-142

Temple, Mary A. 1843 rb-i-484

Tennin, John 1815 rb-b-264

Terrell, McMerran? 1831 rb-f-159

Terrell, Meream 1830 rb-f-136

Terrell, Sally B. 1848 rb-l-132

Terrill, Lewis 1836 rb-g-334

Thaxton, John B. 1855 wb-n-688

Thomas, Elizabeth 1847 rb-k-382

Thomas, Jos. P. 1835 rb-g-236

Thomas, Thomas M. 1849 rb-l-454

Thompson, Elizabeth 1859 rb-p-297

Thompson, John 1831 rb-f-255

Thompson, Lewis 1815 rb-b-250

Thompson, Jane 1845 rb-j-405

Thornton, Owen 1803 rb-a-173

Thornton, Samuel 1813 rb-b-107

Thornton, Orville 1859 rb-p-120

Thornton, Samuel 1813 rb-b-149

Thornton, Samuel 1822 rb-d-32

Thurston, Jno. R. 1848 rb-l-181

Thurston, Monroe? N. 1857 rb-o-495

Tiner, Memory 1833 rb-f-484

Tiner, Noah 1818 rb-b-528

Tinnin, John 1815 rb-b-288

Tire, Thomas 1805 rb-a-238

Tittalson, Mildred 1857 rb-o-525

Titterington, Joseph 1844 rb-j-231

Todd, Sam 1861 rb-p-581

Tolar, John jr. 1835 rb-g-102

Tolar, Wm. W. 1846 rb-k-145

Toler, Isaiah 1853 wb-n-176

Toler, John 1845 rb-j-270

Toler, William 1848 rb-l-48

Totewine, Isaac (Revd.) 1821 rb-c-510

Totewine, Isaac 1821 rb-c-453

Traburn, John 1830 rb-f-139

Tramell, Martha 1855 wb-n-494

Tramell, William 1860 rb-p-386

Tramell, Shadrach 1855 wb-n-628

Travis, John 1827 rb-e-56

Trice, Anderson 1843 rb-j-22

Trice, Edward 1848 rb-l-157

Trice, Elizabeth 1836 rb-g-453

Trice, G. B. 1853 wb-m-657

Trice, Harriett 1841 rb-i-94

Trice, Harriett E. 1849 rb-l-296

Trice, Henry 1851 wb-m-189

Trice, J. B. 1856 rb-o-170

Trice, James 1834 rb-f-568

Trice, Leigh 1848 rb-l-120

Trice, Loranah 1844 rb-j-187

Trice, Lorand 1844 rb-j-120

Trice, Mary 1855 wb-n-674

Trice, May 1855 wb-n-606

Trice, Mindy 1857 rb-o-363

Trice, Nancy 1844 rb-j-264

Trice, Nay 1856 rb-o-145

Trice, Sarah 1854 wb-n-377

Trice, Sarah Ann 1847 rb-k-608

Trice, Susannah 1844 rb-j-82

Trice, Thomas 1846 rb-k-287

Trice, Wilie 1857 rb-o-429

Trice, Willis 1858 rb-o-762

Trice, Zackariah 1848 rb-k-751

Trice, Bingham 1859 rb-p-35

Trice, Edward 1832 rb-f-399

Trice, Edward 1849 rb-l-306

Trice, Ellen W. 1860 rb-p-384

Trice, James 1833 rb-f-462

Trice, James 1834 rb-g-42

Trice, James 1852 wb-m-563

Trice, John 1831 rb-f-215

Trice, Lewis 1842 rb-i-225

Trice, Nace F. 1858 rb-o-583

Trice, Nancy 1848 rb-l-151

Trice, Nay 1856 rb-o-164

Trice, Sally Ann 1849 rb-l-220

Trice, Sarah 1852 wb-m-503

Trice, Shepherd 1840 rb-i-2

Trice, Shepherd 1840 rb-i-25

Trice, Thomas A. 1860 rb-p-429

Trice, Thomas Jackson 1861 rb-p-629

Trigg, George H. 1838 rb-h-78

Trigg, William 1825 rb-d-474

Trigg, William 1838 rb-h-111

Trigg, William 1841 rb-i-74

Trigg, Ann 1838 rb-h-77

Trigg, William 1825 rb-d-477

Trotter, Elizabeth 1831 rb-f-155

Trotter, Isham jr. 1831 rb-f-256

Trotter, Isham sr. 1834 rb-f-579

Trotter, Mary Ann 1859 rb-p-278

Trotter, Robert 1810 rb-a-247

Trotter, Isham 1829 rb-e-406

Trotter, John 1840 rb-h-455

Troville, Henry 1843 rb-i-507

Tubs, Aquilla 1820 rb-c-364

Tubs, Equilla 1818 rb-c-56

Tucker, Curle 1815 rb-b-160

Tully, Guilford 1859 rb-p-33

Turner, William 1849 rb-l-240

Tutt, Mary 1855 wb-n-526

Tyer, Thomas 1821 rb-c-487

Tyler, John D. 1860 rb-p-470

Tyler, William B. 1856 rb-o-22

Tylour, Noah 1818 rb-c-34

Tyner, Memory 1833 rb-f-516

Tyson, Sally 1860 rb-p-501

Tyson, Uriah 1850 wb-m-41

Tyson, William 1860 rb-p-351

Urey, James 1816 rb-b-329

Ury, Isaac 1816 rb-b-361

Ury, Nancy 1823 rb-d-160

Valentine, Charles 1853 wb-n-5

Vance, Elizabeth H. 1858 rb-o-674

Vance, Robert 1829 rb-f-5

Vance, Samuel 1829 rb-f-6

Vance, Samuel B. 1830 rb-f-81

Vance, Saml. 1819 rb-d-190

Vaughan, W. C. 1861 rb-p-615

Vaughan, John P. 1841 rb-i-201

Vaughan, Joshua P. 1829 rb-e-486

Vaughn, James 1858 rb-o-709

Vaughn, W. C. 1858 rb-p-15

Venable, Daniel 1816 rb-b-331

Venable, Daniel 1827 rb-e-76

Vick, Wilson 1858 rb-o-539

Vick, Rowland 1823 rb-d-88

Vineyard, David 1816 rb-b-375

Wagers, James 1822 rb-d-81

Walker, David 1847 rb-k-421

Walker, John 1840 rb-h-386

Walker, Joseph 1847 rb-k-601

Walker, Madison 1853 wb-m-632

Walker, Robert 1846 rb-k-51

Wall, Elijah 1856 rb-o-222

Wall, James C. 1852 wb-m-445

Wall, Johnson (Capt.) 1822 rb-d-97

Wall, Johnson 1822 rb-d-59

Wall, Johnson 1831 rb-f-181

Wall, Charles 1815 rb-b-74

Wall, Johnson 1837 rb-h-38

Wallace, Martha 1831 rb-f-260

Waller, William 1820 rb-c-282

Waller, Robert 1837 rb-g-553

Walton, E. L. 1859 rb-p-279

Walton, Edward 1819 rb-c-216

Walton, William 1817 rb-b-396

Walton, Edward 1820 rb-c-287

Walton, Edward 1820 rb-c-340

Ward, Lucinda Jane 1843 rb-i-518

Warden, Francis H. 1843 rb-i-553

Warfield, James B. 1840 rb-h-420

Warfield, Jane W.? 1838 rb-h-168

Warfield, Laban 1837 rb-g-587

Warfield, Laban 1837 rb-h-61

Warren, S. J. 1848 rb-k-795

Wash, Caty 1825 rb-d-476

Washington, Sally 1841 rb-i-202

Waters, Heneneyra 1860 rb-p-446

Watkins, Benjamin 1815 rb-b-256

Watkins, Henry H. 1841 rb-i-217

Watkins, Henry L. 1846 rb-k-212

Watkins, James 1808 rb-a-81

Watkins, Joseph R. 1856 rb-o-204

Watkins, Benjamin H. 1812 rb-b-100

Watkins, John 1823 rb-d-255

Watson, Allas 1827 rb-e-93

Watson, Henry P. 1860 rb-p-335

Watson, Josiah 1833 rb-f-476

Watson, Wilkins 1858 rb-o-600

Watson, William 1817 rb-b-463

Watt, James 1805 rb-a-274

Watt, James 1817 rb-b-494

Watwood, James 1811 rb-b-15

Watwood, W. (Mrs.) 1856 rb-o-143

Watwood, William 1852 wb-m-544

Weakley, Benjamin 1814 rb-b-196

Weakley, Hannah 1814 rb-b-204

Weakley, Joshua 1836 rb-g-414

Weakley, Margaret 1834 rb-f-543

Weakley, Robert 1816 rb-b-347

Weakley, Robert jr. 1816 rb-b-352

Weakley, Thomas 1831 rb-f-154

Weakley, Isaac 1854 wb-n-363

Weakley, Joshua 1824 rb-d-331

Weakley, Prudence 1855 wb-n-505

Weakley, Samuel 1854 wb-n-339

Weakley, Thomas 1831 rb-f-156

Weakly, John H. 1848 rb-k-799

Weakly, Mary 1847 rb-k-419

Weed, O. 1851 wb-m-249

Welker, Jacob 1844 rb-j-121

Wells, Elisha 1829 rb-e-425

Wells, Martin sr. 1803 rb-a-170

West, Claiborn D. 1861 rb-p-642

West, Elizabeth (Mrs.) 1818 rb-b-514

West, Elizabeth 1817 rb-b-469

West, Elizabeth the elder 1817 rb-b-387

West, George 1810 rb-a-389

Wheatley, Albert G. 1851 wb-m-352

Wheatley, James 1842 rb-i-440

Whelan, James G. 1814 rb-b-193

Wheland, James 1812 rb-b-56

Wheless, Henry 1846 rb-k-269

Wheless, Joseph 1844 rb-j-217

White, Jesse W. 1854 wb-n-432

White, Jim 1854 wb-n-415

White, John 1820 rb-c-386

White, Martha 1847 rb-k-688

White, Mathew 1847 rb-k-507

White, W. S. 1842 rb-i-396

White, William S. 1842 rb-i-417

White, John 1827 rb-e-249

White, William 1808 rb-a-328

Whitehead, William 1836 rb-g-469

Whitehead, Benjamin 1800 rb-a-126

Whitehead, Benjamin 1815 rb-b-166

Whitehead, Benjamin 1837 rb-g-534

Whitfield, Bryan 1825 rb-d-471

Whitfield, Lewis 1838 rb-h-79

Whitfield, Marrie Susan 1855 wb-n-696

Whitfield, Mary 1859 rb-p-110

Whitfield, Mary E. 1851 wb-m-324

Whitfield, Needham 1859 rb-p-278

Whitfield, W. B. 1856 rb-o-154

Whitfield, William B. 1853 wb-n-62

Whitfield, Bryan 1825 rb-d-478

Whitfield, Bryan 1827 rb-e-197

Whitfield, Lewis 1841 rb-i-72

Whitfield, Nathan Bryan 1858 rb-o-710

Whitfield, William B. 1853 wb-n-62

Whitledge, Thomas sr. 1816 rb-b-370

Whitlidge, Thomas 1810 rb-a-347

Whitmill, Drew S. 1819 rb-c-79

Whitsett, John O. 1834 rb-f-542

Whitworth, Elizabeth 1848 rb-k-746

Whitworth, John 1842 rb-i-301

Whitworth, Louiza 1847 rb-k-508

Wickham, Nathan 1854 wb-n-392

Wilcox, Samuel 1821 rb-c-492

Wilcox, John E. 1839 rb-h-281

Wilcox, Samuel 1811 rb-a-380

Wilcox, Samuel Ethelbert 1859 rb-p-142

Wilkerson, George 1816 rb-b-353

Wilkerson, Jehu 1836 rb-g-305

Wilkerson, John 1835 rb-g-233

Wilkinson, Halena 1848 rb-l-179

William, Benjamin 1824 rb-d-311

Williams, D. H. 1855 wb-n-700

Williams, George 1844 rb-j-102

Williams, J. S. 1832 rb-f-327

Williams, Jesse 1836 rb-g-469

Williams, John 1823 rb-d-188

Williams, John 1840 rb-h-381

Williams, John N. 1838 rb-h-30

Williams, John P. 1847 rb-k-617

Williams, Mary 1841 rb-i-207

Williams, Mary W. 1841 rb-i-221

Williams, Mattey 1839 rb-h-333

Williams, Meredith 1826 rb-d-530

Williams, Minnie A. E. 1856 rb-o-97

Williams, Patience 1848 rb-l-126

Williams, William 1854 wb-n-416

Williams, William H. 1837 rb-g-490

Williams, William P. 1857 rb-o-344

Williams, William jr. 1814 rb-b-69

Williams, Charles L. 1859 rb-p-251

Williams, Fielding L. 1845 rb-k-4

Williams, Henry 1827 rb-e-172

Williams, Henry 1851 wb-m-320

Williams, James 1853 wb-n-174

Williams, James 1854 wb-n-211

Williams, Jessee 1836 rb-g-480

Williams, Jno. P. 1854 wb-n-210

Williams, Marrie Ann Elizabeth 1856 rb-o-37

Williams, Mary 1852 wb-m-564

Williams, Septimus 1845 rb-j-446

Williams, Thomas 1849 rb-l-206

Williams, Thomas C. 1848 rb-l-153

Williams, William 1813 rb-b-216

Williamson, John S. 1825 rb-d-450

Williamson, John S. 1834 rb-f-572

Williamson, John T. (S?) 1829 rb-e-470

Williamson, John 1826 rb-d-545

Willis, Elisha 1828 rb-e-273

Willis, Sallie 1855 rb-o-3

Willis, Sarrah E. (Miss) 1856 rb-o-25

Wills, Benjamin D. 1819 rb-c-203

Wills, John L. 1851 wb-m-274

Willson, Polly 1825 rb-d-420

Wilson, Benjamine 1819 rb-c-76

Wilson, Dorothy T. 1852 wb-m-580

Wilson, Hamilton 1847 rb-k-602

Wilson, James 1821 rb-c-542

Wilson, James 1859 rb-p-296

Wilson, John 1819 rb-c-180

Wilson, Sanford 1814 rb-b-176

Wilson, James 1831 rb-f-203

Wilson, Lucy E. 1858 rb-o-585

Wilson, Martha 1820 rb-c-329

Wilson, Samuel 1858 rb-o-565

Wilson, Sandford 1814 rb-b-183

Wilson, Sanford 1848 rb-k-803

Wimberly, Robert H. 1857 rb-o-444

Wimberly, George S. 1857 rb-o-448

Winston, Joseph 1844 rb-j-230

Winters, George 1855 wb-n-495

Wisdom, John M. 1858 rb-o-779

Wood, James B. 1860 rb-p-446

Wood, Miland 1841 rb-i-103

Wood, James 1845 rb-j-393

Wood, Mary 1845 rb-j-393

Wood, Miland 1841 rb-i-116

Woodmore, James W. 1839 rb-h-334

Woods, J. B. 1860 rb-p-472

Woodson, Joseph 1855 wb-n-658

Woolfork, Joseph 1831 rb-f-227

Wootten, Polly 1825 rb-d-419

Wootten, Mary 1825 rb-d-426

Word, Seth 1845 rb-j-350

Worrell, Thomas 1838 rb-h-125

Worrell, Thomas 1839 rb-h-222

Worthington, Ann 1849 rb-l-358

Wray, Joseph 1819 rb-c-136

Wray, Nathan 1806 rb-a-443

Wright, James T. 1843 rb-j-19

Wright, James Y. 1849 rb-l-423

Wright, Susanna G. 1845 rb-j-459

Wright, William 1840 rb-h-458

Wyatt, Thomas 1855 rb-o-1

Wyatt, Sarrah 1856 rb-o-40

Wynne, George 1845 rb-j-406

Yancy, William 1810 rb-b-142

Yarbrough, John 1855 wb-n-571

Yarbrough, Mary (Mrs) 1858 rb-o-577

Yarbrough, Mary 1860 rb-p-458

Yarbrough, Moses 1840 rb-i-22

Yarbrough, Nancie 1858 rb-o-540

Yarbrough, George 1847 rb-k-323

Yates, Belfield C. 1859 rb-p-18

Yates, James G. 1845 rb-j-430

Yates, Willie B. 1848 rb-k-745

Young, Ann O. (Martin) 1839 rb-h-272

Young, Nancy O. 1839 rb-h-220

Young, Dorrell 1823 rb-d-211